a treasury
of motorcycles
of the world

about the author

Floyd Clymer is the author of *Treasury of Early American Automobiles, History of American Steam Automobiles, History of All Indianapolis Races, A Treasury of Foreign Automobiles,* and *Henry's Wonderful Model T,* among others. He has written and/or published 400 titles on automotive subjects. Clymer literally grew up with motorcycles, as he began to ride at the age of eleven. He started amateur racing at fifteen, was a professional and a dealer at seventeen, and has won many national championships. He is the publisher of *Cycle* magazine—a monthly publication about motorcycles.

floyd clymer

a treasury
of motorcycles
of the world

Bonanza Books • New York

a treasury of motorcycles of the world
517091208
Copyright © MCMLXV by Floyd Clymer. All Rights Reserved.
Printed in the United States of America.
This book, or parts thereof, may not be reproduced
in any form without permission of the publishers.
Library of Congress Catalog Card Number: 65-26164

This edition published by Bonanza Books,
a division of Crown Publishers, Inc.,
by arrangement with McGraw-Hill Book Company, Inc.

(I)

In memory of Oscar Hedstrom, inventor of the Indian
motorcycle, and George M. Hendee, founder and first
president of the Indian Company, and to the three
Davidson brothers, William, Walter and Arthur,
and their partner, William S. Harley. Indian was the
first. Harley-Davidson, also a pioneer, still in
business, is the only remaining mass producer
of motorcycles in the United States.

how it all started

Indian was the first mass producer of motorcycles in the United States, and nearly 100 different makes have been manufactured since the inception of the industry. During the 1930's the sales of motorcycles in the United States declined, and in the 1950's, Indian, as an American manufacturer at Springfield, Massachusetts, discontinued production. The Indian name was then placed on A.J.S. and later on Royal-Enfield bikes built in England. In the early 1960's motorcycles bearing the Indian name were no more.

In early years a few different makes of foreign motorcycles were imported, mostly British, a few German and Italian, but no Japanese. It was, however, just prior to World War II that sizable quantities of foreign makes were imported and the interest in foreign motorcycles increased. After World War II the foreign motorcycle popularity increased by leaps and bounds, and in the late 1950's when Honda came in with an extensive advertising program, sales really started to soar.

For many years Harley-Davidson and Indian alone had to carry the burden of motorcycle advertising in this country. When Indian sales declined, the entire U.S. sales promotion efforts for motorcycles were almost exclusively through the efforts of Harley-Davidson. For many years the sales of motorcycles in the United States remained about the same each year, with perhaps an increase or decline of about 10 per cent from year to year. How things have changed!

Floyd Clymer

credits

Our thanks to the many individuals and firms that helped to make this book possible by contributing photographs, news items, articles and other necessary information. Among those are Harley-Davidson Motor Company, Larry Wise, Honda Motor Company, Yamaha International Corporation, B.S.A. Western, Pete Colman, Johnson Motors, Inc., Don J. Brown, B.S.A. Incorporated, Ted Hodgdon, Webco, Emmett Moore, Lyn Abrams, Paul Halesworth, Bob Bates, Action Sports, Grant Whidden, Shell Oil Company, Lester Nehamkin, Kim Kimball, Daytona International Speedway, Bill France, *Motor Cycling, The Motorcycle, Motorcycle News, Motorcycle Journal,* Ralph Poole, Jack Mercer, Lynn Wineland, Ray Garner, Cliff Boswell, Fred Stebbins, *Motorcyclist,* Bill Bagnall, Bert Brundage, J. C. Agajanian, Lin Kuchler and Jules Horky of the American Motorcycle Association, Walter von Schonfeld of AAMRR, Marvin Foster, Bob Hicks, Boyd Reynolds, Herb Ottoway, Alf Child, Motokov, Berliner Corporation, Frank Cooper, Bob Greene, Pete Peters, Montesa, Cemoto-Bultaco, Triumph Corporation, Al Bondy, Earl Flanders, U.S. Suzuki, Jack McCormack, Zelda Buck, Cliff Buxton, John Gilbride, Al Melanson, Nick Nicholson, Jim Greening, Bill Newrock, Roxy Rockwood, William Grapevine, Ron White, G. Luraschi, Allen Friedrich, John Gontner, John Pitts, John Gregoire, Robert Armstrong, James McGowan, Dustin Frazer, and Javier Lopez.

We are sorry if there is someone we have overlooked. It was not intentional.

contents

How It All Started

today

yesterday

a treasury
of motorcycles
of the world

today

Gleaming Triumph symbolizes adult world of power for fascinated small boy. (Left)

Many a male ego has been deflated by the skill of today's motorcycling miss. Attractive girls enjoy cycling, such as this young lady on a Jawa. (Below)

Welcome. Welcome to the new era of motorcycling. Whether you are a long-time enthusiast or just curious, there is much here to enjoy.

To prove this is truly a new era, one has merely to look around, not only at the number of motorcycles now in use, but at the caliber of people using them. Even the statistical figures bear this out: Here in America there was an increase just after the Second World War, to about one-half million riders. California led the nation with over 60,000, nearly twice as many as Illinois, Pennsylvania, and Texas, each with close to 30,000. Ohio and New York were not far behind. Then nearly 20 per cent dwindled away in the following six years before it began climbing again. At that time the machines began noticeably improving in suspension and appearance. The European importers began pushing harder, and by 1957 things were back to normal, going even higher in 1958. The year 1961 was a landmark year, some 200,000 were registered, and this is approximately where the phenomenal upsurge made its initial appearance. The Japanese began making huge inroads on a virgin market with heavy advertising expenditures. They had a new concept of motorcycling and marketing. They were ignoring the genuine, "hard-core" cyclist and aiming at the non-rider: those who had not ridden before but who would be intrigued by the small, quiet, inexpensive machines. In 1961, Japan exported over 23,000 motorcycles to the U.S.; as many as the next importer, Italy, with 13,000, and third-place Austria with 12,000 (nearly all were Allstate made for Sears Roebuck & Company by Puch of

Austria). England was fourth with 8,000. However, England was on top in dollar value: nearly $4 million of machines and another million dollars in parts.

The year 1962 was another boom year; California held its lead, the pinpoint target of the "new wave" ad program, registering 102,030. Texas had nearly half as many, and for the U.S. figures were up to 650,000. This does not include those that were used off the road, and racing motorcycles, which might add another 10 per cent and which were not licensed for highway use. Next year, 1963, imports jumped to a total of 183,351, with Japan accounting for 135,469, and a dollar volume of $24,555,000. England was second with 15,672 and over $7 million. Total

Representative of motorcycling's new image is this bright, well-stocked sales/service store in Glendale, California. Literally hundreds of such attractive facilities are springing up each year.

registration in the U.S. surpassed 770,000. So it has grown, by leaps and bounds to the present, where late in 1964 the one million mark was passed. The coming years have even greater expectations. A careful survey indicates that within three years, the motorcycling population will be *eight times* as great as in 1960. Figuring that for every motorcycle registered, there are approximately five riders, there would currently be about 5 million cyclists in the U.S. By 1968 this number should easily top 9,000,000.

Even *Life* magazine, with typical conservatism, estimates over 3,000,000 riders at the present time.

By 1970 Southern California alone is predicted to have over a million, the hotbed of motorcycling activity. This area claims several thousand *registered* sport competition riders, most of whom have *un*registered motorcycles.

The people who ride them, of course, are largely responsible for the growth, and here too, an insight of the new image proves interesting. Since the days in 1885 when Gottlieb Daimler invented the first practical motorcycle it has attracted the adventurous ones. Unfortunately this included, in America, some that used the motorcycle for the wrong type of recognition and this group cast an undesirable picture of the sport. However, since the boom of the lightweight motorcycle the predominance of people is altogether different. This has snowballed to include the very prominent influential people of society and the entertainment world, doctors, lawyers and artists.

Modern business people are known to their associates as regularly cycling to meetings or luncheons while carrying briefcases—a solution to the traffic, as well as providing an exhilarating break from office routine.

Sportsmen accepted the motorcycle quite readily when the specialized trail machines were introduced. Now they had a trustworthy mount to get them to their off-the-road areas, and very economically, too! Women also realize the joys of motorcycling—like Mrs. Chet Huntley, who received one for her birthday from her husband, the well-known New York commentator. She uses her lightweight to get about quickly in the tight traffic of New York City. Another cycling New Yorker is Dr. Seymour Hutchinson, a dental surgeon who rides 64 miles a day to and from his office in Brooklyn. The doctor has also tried his hand at competition and was very successful. New York even has its own elite cycle organization in the Madison Avenue Motorcycle Club with members including writers, lawyers, editors, jewelers and actors. On the West Coast, many notables from the acting profession are avid cycling enthusiasts. One of the most outspoken is Steve McQueen, who has had a try at international cycling competition, and has had his hobby a prominent part of features articles on him in *Life* and *Harper's Bazaar*. Beautiful Janet Leigh and Ann Margret enjoy the sport of riding, as does singer Dean Martin. Marlon Brando is a veteran of nearly twenty years on two wheels, as is actor Keenan Wynn. Auto racing drivers are also riders and/or owners such as A. J. Foyt, Dan Gurney,

Today's motorcycle salespeople are (generally) neat, helpful, courteous. Enthusiasts themselves, they will go out of their way to instruct the new owner—be he high school sophomore or affluent businessman. (Left) Two-wheelers are very big with adventure-lovers. (Below)

The motorcyclist is free to roam at will through wild and splendid back country never seen by the average tourist.

Jim Hurtubise, Lloyd Ruby, Paul Goldsmith, Joe Leonard and many others.

Popularity continues, and more and more join in. Television commercials now show knowledgeable Americans on motorcycles. Movies and books are cast where the hero is a cyclist. Suddenly cycling is "in," accepted as family fun. FBI Director J. Edgar Hoover points out in a statement, "Your Motorcycle and You," that "Simple courtesy is the key to acceptance, and motorcycle clubs, as well as individual owners, by adhering to a rigid code of courteous conduct, can do much to add to the safety of the highway." He also states, "The care you exercise in handling your motorcycle at all times will add to the safety of our streets and highways. It will also increase the pride and pleasure you take in an activity which, in many cases, is more than just a sport and more than just a hobby."

There is another example of the people now cycling, perhaps one of the more enlightening ones. A Baptist minister, the Reverend Mr. James Campbell, uses his to visit his parishioners and travel to Bible conferences. The preacher feels his cycle brings him closer to the youth of his church.

These men and women are just some of the people in the new era of motorcycles. Combine these with the old stalwarts that have been with it all these years and you begin to realize that large as it is, it has just begun. Just begun to grow and just begun to be enjoyed. After all, cycling is a many varied sport.

The new Honda "90."

The first we heard of the Japanese Honda was when an U.S. Air Force Captain stationed in Japan sent us some interesting photos and a short story about Mr. S. Honda and his motorcycle factory. This was about 1955. Through correspondence, in the fall of 1958 arrangements were made for the company to send the first Honda to come into the United States to *Cycle* magazine for a road test which appeared in the December, 1958 issue. The machine attracted a great deal of attention and had some unique features. Honda then started their advertising campaign, which was to become a fantastic one, by using 12 full-page ads in *Cycle* magazine. The first ads were prepared in Japan, used many Japanese characters and were typical Japanese ads which later were revised and written to appeal to the American market. *Cycle* had the first advertising schedule that Honda placed in the United States and the ads appeared in no other U.S. publications. As a result of interest created and the letters and telegrams from U.S. dealers and enthusiasts, Honda decided to open a U.S. branch. Mr. K. Kawashima, who was to become the Managing Director in the United States, came from Japan. Mr. William Hunt, who had been in the Air Force in Japan, was with him, and in our first talk they announced their plans for entering the U.S. market. At the time their sales promotions ideas seemed fantastic and seemingly unobtainable. They first considered having their main offices in Houston, Texas, apparently because the port facilities there seemed most desirable. I suggested, however, that Houston was a long distance from the major markets in the United States and they should locate either on the East or West Coast or in Chicago or Detroit. Their decision later was to locate in Los Angeles where they started and later built a very fine building in nearby Gardena where U.S. Honda business is handled today.

At first there appeared to be some resentment among many U.S. dealers feeling that Honda would cut into their business. What actually happened was that Honda, through their advertising and promotional efforts, helped to create a new interest in the motorcycle business which resulted in increased business for motorcycle importers and dealers in competitive makes. Honda established many new dealers that previously had been in other lines of business and, in some instances, the Honda line added to already established businesses of other lines. Honda must be given credit for the increased popularity and sales boom that now exists in the industry. Through their efforts, other Japanese makes started to sell in large quantities. Foreign makes from other countries continue to gain in popularity and sales. Certainly no one could foresee the fantastic growth of Honda and the sales they have been able to secure in the United States. For the past year they have sold in the United States about 70 per cent as many Hondas as Volkswagen has cars. Now most U.S. motorcycle dealers, even though they may handle competitive makes, praise Honda for their efforts. One importer once remarked to me, "We should be eternally grateful to Honda."—F.C.

*The 1958 ads that started Honda's
fabulous advertising campaign in
America first appeared in Cycle
magazine.*

One way of transporting several lightweight or trail machines is to load them securely in pick-up. Tailgate should close. Overload springs (though not essential) help level ride. (Left)

Many enthusiasts buy or build 2- or 3-rail trailer which reduces loading and travel problems to a minimum. (Center)

Lucky Wheels Club is representative of well-knit groups in which members dress and equip similarly. They are on Death Valley (California) Annual Tour. (Below)

Many motorcyclists are members of motorcycle clubs who enjoy riding together on vacations and just for fun. There are also small groups of cyclists who are not members of any organized club but who enjoy riding with their friends for fun, health and recreation.

Largest annual rally is famous Death Valley Tour with rendezvous at Furnace Creek Ranch. Over 2,500 rode in for 10th celebration.

500-Mile Greenhorn Enduro takes name from rugged mountain range; is long-established, highly organized event shown by Pasadena (California) Motorcycle Club. (Top)

Very popular desert enduros are competitive events over rugged terrain that test men and machines to their limits. (Center)

Organizing small events is easy; major clubs and associations aid neighborhood groups with information. (Bottom)

Refueling from a can in a desert contest—just like the old days—as girl mechanic checks something for her guy.

Bigger every year, the Bill Johnson Invitational Road Rally brings together hundreds of Southern California riders. (Above)

High and beautiful Sierra Juarez country in Mexico rewards riders in Bill Robertson's yearly "Baja-liday" group tour. (Right)

Most motorcycle dealers can provide new owners with insurance information and application forms. Two-wheeler magazines carry advertising of most insurance firms specializing in this field. A.M.A. Competition Committee member and dealer Aub LeBard on left. (Top)

Lightweight trail machines emphasize shield on high-rise exhaust pipe to prevent possible leg burns; a "good citizen" feature on many is spark arrestor to prevent forest fires when riding in wooded country back roads.

LOW-COST INDEMNITY IS A BY-PRODUCT OF A SAFE SPORT

An excellent example of the new, improved image of motorcycles can be found in the fields of financing and insurance. These businesses are known for their practical methods, and their acceptance of motorcycles is another mark on the bonus ledger of the sport.

Banks, finance companies, and credit unions consider motorcycles "safe risks," and offer excellent services to the customer. Many will offer up to the full amount of the purchase price. They also play a large part in the dealer business by flooring his stock, and a portion even accommodate some return to the dealer for sending his customers their way. Of course, the reason for all this lies in the sound fact that motorcycle people have proven solvent, solid citizens. Evidence of this is supported by the fact that about 80 per cent of current new sales are paid in cash. Other dealers themselves have a time-payment plan, usually a short-term affair with a substantial down payment, receiving a few dollars for their investment.

In the area of insurance protection, there are some distinct advantages for the cyclist. For example, there are no additional premiums for age categories; hence some young people find they can afford a motorcycle just from the savings on insurance!

The majority of neighborhood cycle stores have access to liberal financing plans—up to 100 per cent has been advanced by banks and financial institutions on motorcycles to good credit risks. (Bottom)

As in the auto field, motorcycles have coverage for liability, fire and theft, and also for the uninsured motorist. This latter coverage is as low as only $1.50 per month additional in any category. Liability is based on engine displacement, with four categories: up to 66cc, 67 to 180cc, 181 to 328cc, and over 328cc. In the lowest range, $32 per year buys $2500 bodily injury each person, and $50,000 each accident, property damage $10,000 each accident and $25 deductible. In higher ranges it goes up, with premium of $42.00, $54.00, $68.00 for the same coverage. Even lower rates and limits are available. Coverage for the motorcycle itself is based on the cost of the machine including extra equipment. For basic fire and theft with $25 deductible, the yearly price is $16. This is the coverage that finance companies require to protect their loan. To add $50 deductible collision insurance, raise the low rate to $64. So, if the motorcycle actually sold, complete, for $600, the rate would be $120.

These policies would apply to street machines in stock condition. Coverage for customs for liability is available, but not fire and theft. One other point, racing, or entry in competitive sporting events, or even cow trailing is not included in the coverage.

Insurance laws may differ in many states, as do rates.

There are many different methods used by instructors in teaching a new rider how to properly operate a motorcycle. In many instances the beginner does not receive proper instruction and/or does not have a long enough period of lessons.

The methods outlined below are those used by successful dealers and/or ones with long connection with motorcycling or the motorcycle business. Any of the methods if studied and applied will help the new rider to become more proficient. — Floyd Clymer.

by TED HODGDON
President, BSA, Incorporated
Nutley, New Jersey

During World War II it was my privilege to write the manual for the U.S. Armed Forces entitled "How to Ride a Motorcycle on Rough Terrain— That Is, Sand, Mud, Gravel, Etc." Before that I had taught literally hundreds of people to ride motorcycles, and I think I can sum it up pretty clearly in the following:

(1) Ask if the prospect knows how to ride a bicycle, but regardless of his reply, ask him to sit on the machine and give him a short push. Tell him to lift his feet as soon as you start pushing, place them on the footrests and steer the machine —that is, balance it. A twenty-foot push will tell you right away whether this man can balance the machine easily and naturally. If he cannot, you have a bicycle teaching job to do; if he can, you are ready to start the engine.

(2) *Don't* start the engine for him. Show him the action of the controls, and *let him start the engine.*

No matter how petite the rider, perfect balance can be achieved by combination of proper machine size and instruction. This is a light Ducati ridden by model Gloria Dee.

Instructor directs new rider to change gears, turn, slow, stop in safety of large vacant lot. (Left)

Without starting engine, new rider gets feeling of proper balance while being pushed on his lightweight by friend or instructor. (Below)

Early lesson in engine starting: instructor directs the beginner from safe position where he can watch foot and hand actions. (Bottom)

(3) Show him the working of the throttle and emphasize over and over again that you turn the throttle *outward,* away from you, to slow down. (4) Now show him the clutch, the hand clutch and brake levers. Show him that by merely squeezing both of them, he can come to a gentle stop. (5) Whatever you do, don't start to teach a man to ride on a gravel sandy patch. Don't teach him to ride on macadam or paved road that has loose sand or gravel on it. The best plan is to take him onto a ball ground such as a grassy field or other open area and tell him to ride in a large circle. (6) After you are sure that he understands the working of the controls and he can *show* you the position of the foot brake, the hand brake and the clutch lever, and repeat to you and demonstrate that he knows the action of the throttle—that turning it *outward away from him* slows down the machine, you are then ready to have him squeeze the hand clutch, put it into low gear and get started. (7) Give him strict instructions *not* to shift gears, in fact *you don't even want to tell him how to get into second gear until you have seen him ride in low gear.* However, he must be shown how to get back into neutral in case he stalls the machine while away from you and must then restart. (8) *Now,* before this man starts off from where you are standing, tell him this, which is one of the greatest fundamentals I know of in riding a motorcycle and staying out of trouble. That is, "Never turn around in a roadway—never turn around at all—until you have *turned your head completely over your shoulder.*" In an automobile you may look

15

Starting early! Motorcycle dealer's son tries first backyard solo. May grow up to be a national champion!

Motorcycles with automatic transmissions usually substitute a rear brake lever for familiar clutch lever of standard machines, such as this Honda "55" Model. (Right)

New rider is shown "double squeeze" method of stopping: left hand controls clutch; right, brake. (Left)

Relaxed but attentive to road conditions, this rider demonstrates the correct "upright" posture. (Opposite page)

in a mirror or just turn your head sideways, but on a motorcycle that is not enough. You must turn your head completely over your shoulder and look to see if there are any cars coming. (9) Once the chap has circled the field in low, several times, and has shown you he can slow down and start up by the use of the throttle, teach him to stop and start about a dozen times. (10) *Then*—and only then—are you in a position to show him how to get into second gear, third gear and fourth gear.

by FRANK H. COOPER
Royal-Enfield Distributor
Los Angeles, California

FIRST: Take the person for a ride at moderate speeds and give him warning before leaning the motorcycle down on corners. Show him the operation of each control separately and explain that when the clutch is disengaged you have nothing more to do to stop than to apply the brakes. *With the clutch disengaged*, rev the engine

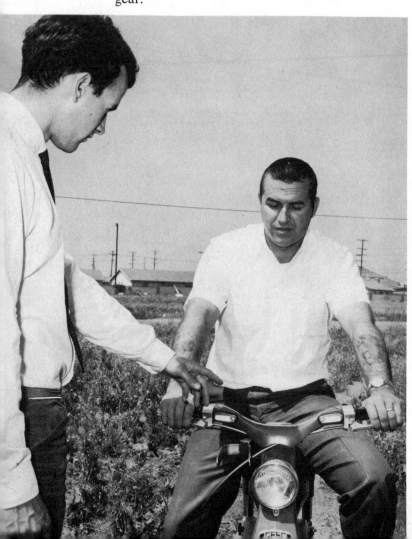

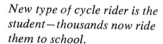
New type of cycle rider is the student—thousands now ride them to school.

fast a few times to show the student that regardless of what the engine is doing, you will have the same thing as a bicycle if the clutch is disengaged.

SECOND: Place the motorcycle on the center stand with a 2 x 6, or equivalent, under the stand in order to raise the rear wheel off the ground. Start the engine and have the student get aboard the motorcycle. Now, teach the student, thoroughly, the operation of the clutch in coordination with the throttle; then teach him the shifting of the gears and how to find neutral. Let him practice for quite some time. Now teach him the easiest method of starting the motorcycle and the operation of the throttle when starting the engine. Explain that when starting the engine, the rider should have his gears in neutral.

THIRD: Take the student for his first dual instruction and try to sit as far forward as possible so that the student can reach the controls. Teach the student one control at a time. While driving in second or third gear, have the student practice engaging the clutch while you rev up the motor a bit, so that he can get the feel of engaging the clutch smoothly. Next, have the student operate the throttle while *you* operate the clutch and shift gears. It is not best that the student have both hands on the handlebars. You still need to be master of the motorcycle. Now let him get back to operating the clutch again, and let him also shift gears while *you* operate the throttle.

FOURTH: The student should now be ready for his first solo ride. Pick out a long section of street that is seldom used, or an empty lot. Impress on the student that, with the clutch disengaged, you

have the same thing as a bicycle. Have the student practice starting and stopping the motorcycle by *just barely letting the clutch take contact* and quickly disengaging it so that the machine moves only a few feet before stopping. This is very important and should be done at least a half dozen times before the student starts to solo. Instruct the student to stop at the end of the street and put the gearbox into neutral, then for him to get off of the motorcycle (keeping the engine running) and walk the motorcycle around, ready for the return trip. Remind the student to take it slow and practice shifting gears, but not to get into high gear at low speeds. Remind him again to *use the clutch if the motor should jerk or if he wants to stop.*

I have taught hundreds of people to ride and I have been very successful with the above routine. The new riders have confidence in themselves when they first ride alone.

Reaction time in emergency is reduced to minimum by a motorcycling exclusive: Clutch lever is always in rider's grasp on most bikes. (Far left)

Proper use of front brake. (Top)

Left hand gives rider instant control of clutch lever. Horn button is within reach of thumb. (Bottom)

by HAP JONES
Distributor, Motorcycle Accessories
San Francisco, California

I like the idea of the Teach-a-Rider Contest very much and I'm very glad to give my method for teaching new riders how to operate a motorcycle.

First I have a talk with the rider and determine his ability to ride a bicycle or drive an automobile. Then explain the controls in detail and demonstrate the actual operation of the motorcycle by showing him the starting procedure, the operation of the clutch, the gearshift and the location of the brake. This is done without riding the machine more than a few feet. When I am sure that he understands the controls sufficiently, I have him mount the machine and instruct him to start riding in low gear, usually in a small area and never more than around the block. In the event he kills the engine and cannot get started again, I am nearby to help him. From then on it is just a matter of practicing starting and stopping and shifting gears until he is capable of controlling the machine properly.

One of the most important steps in teaching a new rider is to get him to relax and convince him that the main difference in operating a motorcycle over an automobile is the gas control. Too, a new rider should be instructed in a quiet, slow manner so that you do not excite him, and the operation should be explained to him as briefly and simply as possible. Every effort should be made to put the rider at ease so that he is in a relaxed mood when he starts riding. Should you find that

your pupil becomes tense and excited, or that he is afraid of the traffic, it is advisable to give him lessons where there is the minimum of traffic.

I never mount the machine with the pupil while he is at the controls. If you find a man who is slow in learning, it is advisable to have him ride with you as a passenger so that he can watch all the controls and how the motorcycle is handled.

I have taught hundreds of riders by this method and found it most satisfactory.

by EARL ROBINSON
Harley-Davidson Dealer
Detroit, Michigan

I have been showing people how to ride motorcycles for 27 years now and failed only once. One fellow was impossible. I finally got him to the point where he rode the bike home through traffic, but he never took it out of the garage again.

I have found that it is generally a good thing if you can divide the lesson into two separate periods on different days. No riding the first day. Merely put the motorcycle on the stand, if it has a rear one, and show the student how to start it and go through the gears a few times. When he comes back in a day or so, he is not nearly so nervous and he has the procedure pretty well in mind. I try to make him feel as much at ease as possible by telling him there isn't anything he can hurt by shifting wrong, etc. If I have any doubts, I set the throttle so it won't open very far, if the type motorcycle makes that possible.

Famous competition men, Ed Kretz, Jr., Ed Kretz, Sr., and Pete Colman. Pete is now BSA Western General Manager. He was once a Triumph man.

After showing him all I can with the motorcycle standing still, I start him riding. I tell him to keep his eyes absolutely to the front when starting out, and not to do any shifting, but to go about a block, stop, put it in neutral, get off, and push the bike around. After observing his reactions I use my judgment as to when to let him shift into higher gears, turn corners, etc.

Another thing I always tell a student is, that if he should open the throttle and not be able to shut it off, to step on the brake hard and stall the motor.

by JACK MERCER
Roadman, The Triumph Corporation
Towson, Baltimore, Maryland

The method I favor is first to take the new prospect for a brief spin, being careful *not to frighten* him, or her, as the case might be. There is no cause for showing off. More persons have been scared off cycles by that one-and-only experience when some nut gave them a "Marlon Brando" treatment! Just recall what a thrill your first ride was on a motorcycle and remember the same thrill is being experienced by the person on the saddle behind you. I think it equally important to find a fairly deserted strip of road so that the prospect can *relax*.

The second brief hop, with me still at the controls, is repeated, but this time a general briefing is given on the various controls. The novice is permitted to twirl the throttle, just to help build

up his interest. Spin number 3 is done with me on the back and the newcomer at the bars, but my hands are also up front—just in case. Once it has been determined that the person has a satisfactory understanding of the controls, a short *first-gear-only* hop is permitted, with the newcomer doing an actual solo ride and me trotting along beside.

The final solo ride with full instructions from starting to shifting through all gears, and a turn in the highway is the completion of the test. In general, almost anyone of normal intelligence can be checked out for a first solo ride on the middleweight motorcycles in less than one hour.

by ED KRETZ
Winner of
Ten National Championships
Motorcycle Dealer
Monterey Park, California

I used the following procedure when I taught riding at the Ordnance Base in Pomona, California, during World War II.

I always would teach the rider how to start the engine and shift the gears as the first part of the instruction period. Then I would have them sit on the machine while on the stand with the engine running. This would enable them to get used to the throttle, working it back and forth. Then I would explain that they should not run the engine at too slow a speed in the higher gears and also that it was always necessary to shift to a lower gear when the engine impulse or chain jerk would occur.

I would also instruct them to watch carefully at intersections, while riding on the highway, for cars which might make a left hand turn in front of them. And I constantly emphasized that they should always glance back over their shoulders and hold out their hands when making turns in either direction, or when stopping. Sometimes, in the Army course, I would suggest that the beginner ride very slowly, and we even had some slow races so that the operator could learn to keep his balance better.

I believe that the information that the beginner needs to operate his motorcycle is also very important in helping him to have confidence in himself, so that the time spent operating the machine on the stand and learning thoroughly the operation of the controls, is very important, and will pay off fully when he takes his first solo ride.

by EARL FLANDERS
Flanders Co., Pasadena, California
Western District BMW Motorcycles—
Accessory Manufacturers

In brief, my method of teaching a new rider is as follows: I first take him for a ride through a quiet, uncongested area, showing him the different procedures: starting and shifting a motorcycle, with myself riding in front. Then I stop and go over the routine with the motorcycle stationary. After that I get on in back, and, letting him lean slightly forward with his hand on the handlebars, just in front of the controls, we go through the routine of starting, stopping and shifting the motorcycle again. After that, I let him put his hands and feet on the controls and repeat the same operations, doing this three or four times from a standing start to running in fourth gear. After he has gone through these operations and I feel he has become somewhat familiar with the handling of the machine, I then have him ride around the block several times by himself, each time stopping him and giving advice and corrections.

Usually, after two or three trips around the block sufficient confidence is instilled to enable the average rider to go off on his own for a day or two. After he returns, we review all the procedures, and I take a ride on the back, pointing out some of the hazards of riding a motorcycle, such as: staying in the middle of a lane and not on the right-hand side; watching for newspaper and sand on the corners; bringing out the fact of being careful with the front-wheel brake any time he is in a turn. I usually stress the fact about the front wheel brake by asking him to use only 1 or 2 fingers on the front wheel brake when in a corner. At other times, when making a straight-line stop, he can use his whole hand.

by BOB SCHANZ
Sport Motors, Cincinnati, Ohio

It is an excellent idea and something that should have been done long ago. Congratulations on another "first" for *Cycle!* When I teach a new rider to operate a motorcycle or scooter I begin during the actual sales pitch. The early familiari-

zation with the operation puts the prospective customer (and often his parents also) at ease and makes him more anxious for a demonstration ride.

So the procedure goes like this: (1) Showing the main features of the machine in question such as brakes, gearshift, clutch, etc. Demonstrate their operation in such a way that the beginner prospect will have the control layout already digested before he ever sits on the model. (2) During the demonstration ride you call the beginner's attention to the operation of all controls so that while you are explaining the merits of the smooth operation, etc., you are actually showing him how they work. (3) Give the learner a "dry run" on starting procedures and gear shifting with the machine on the stand. Then there follows an actual firing up of the model. (4) There is a large parking lot behind our store where we generally let them loose for the first time. The beginner has by this time mastered starting and engaging first cog. I then let him make a couple of slow laps around the lot in first gear. While this is in progress I instruct him in the correct operation of both brakes. (5) When he has learned to start from a standstill, ride off in first gear and return and stop and select neutral, I refresh his memory on hitting the higher gears and let him have a go at that. When he has made numerous up-and-down gear changes, starts and stops, I teach him how to make an emergency stop without dropping or stalling the bike. (6) I then turn the beginner loose in traffic for a few cautious trips around the block. After I am satisfied that he understands everything I let him go on his own.

by SKIP FORDYCE
Riverside, California
Harley-Davidson, Triumph,
Honda Dealer

I have used the following method in teaching over 3,000 students without an accident. I suggest that the student sit on the regular seat and the instructor on the tank ahead of the student and use the following procedure:

1. STEERING: Place both your hands on the handlebars with your fingers and hands extended flat (do not wrap or grip the bars). Then I put my hands right on top of yours and when I say "right" we push to the right, say "left" we push to the left. *The machine always goes the way you push the handlebar.*

2. GAS CONTROL: Close both hands loosely over their respective handlebars, all the time with my hands on top of yours. Then I show you how the gas control works by saying "on," "off," and you will take a reaction from my hand which is guiding yours to control the throttle.

3. BRAKES: Then to the brakes, lightly cushioning on the rear brake and letting it up until you get the feel of that brake. Then the front wheel brake the same way, also teaching you how to

Two-year-old Donny Droud of Lincoln, Nebraska (wearing racing helmet) sits atop one of his father's racing bikes at Dodge City, Kansas.

spool off the throttle as you put on the front wheel brake. Then we put the two brakes together.

4. CLUTCH: Whether it is a foot clutch or hand clutch, I have you release it, let it coast a few feet, pull it in and out, etc.

5. SHIFTING: Put your foot on the foot shift, and I do the clutching and operate the gas control; you just do the shifting.

6. LEFT TURN WITH HAND SIGNAL: Let hand off the bar, pull up with the right hand instead of pushing. This also allows you to make a shift with the hand gearshift model.

7. PUT THE PREVIOUS 6 TOGETHER IN THE FOLLOWING ORDER: Roll along at 12 or 15 miles an hour and *you* go through the entire procedure of shutting the gas off, pull the clutch, make the shift, let the clutch back out again and turn the gas back on. Both up gear and down gear, never below 10 miles an hour. Then several blocks of real slow speed riding, just enough to keep the motorcycle going, around 3 to 10 miles an hour, then weave the machine from side to side while still going slowly.

8. STOPPING AND STARTING: I am still sitting on the gas tank. You make the stop and I drop my feet onto the ground, holding the motorcycle up. However, my hands are still on top of yours, just in case you should let the clutch out or turn the gas on. After a couple of perfect stops, you are ready to drop *your* feet onto the ground and make the complete stop with no help from me.

9. GET OFF THE MOTORCYCLE AND PUSH MOTORCYCLE IN A CIRCLE.

10. OVERTAKING AND PASSING A CAR: On the machine again, me up on the gas tank. You must relax your fingers and hands from around the handlebars so that you can turn and look over either shoulder. This eliminates pressure on handlebars when turning your head, and when your eyes come back to the road you will be in the same spot in the road you were before you turned your head. *You are now ready to solo— but before you do, read the following! Don't assume yourself to death:* Let us bear in mind that *motorcycles are proved to be the safest means of transportation on the highways in California—*

But—Statistics prove that 62 per cent of *those few* that have been killed on motors have met their deaths in either of two different types of accidents, *both at intersections.* (*Don't* get the impression that 62 per cent of all riders get killed.)

Let's take these two in order.

NUMBER ONE: A boulevard stop sign. Do not confuse this with the red, green and yellow flasher signals. The one to *really* beware of is the ordinary octagon-shaped (in California) stop sign on the side streets or the open highway. Let's drive down an ordinary boulevard lined with these stop signs, whether it is in town, especially on side streets, or out on the open highway.

You, on your motorcycle, see an automobile coming up to the stop, and because of your unlimited visibility, *you immediately see him.* Now let's get behind the steering wheel of the automobile and see what I mean by you motorcycle riders *assuming yourself to death.* The car driver approaches the stop sign. He is not in heavy

Ride-the-plank, or a teeter-totter contest, is always interesting. Plank balancing act amuses and instructs at the same time.

traffic conditions so he takes a casual look to the left and to the right, driving all this time by *reflex* or *remote* action. He is looking for a car on the boulevard or on the highway. He sees none *because his mind actually* is on the radio, the heater, the windshield wipers, or his job or school-work that he is going to, or his family he has just left or is hurrying home to. There may be other complications of glare, dirt on the windowpanes around him, a post sticking up in front of him, a cigarette that has burned a little bit too closely to the falling-off point in the ash tray, or any one of many other things that could distract his attention. Well—he takes a quick look, and *looks right through you,* just as though you were a ghost. He either makes a milkman's stop, or makes a complete stop and then drives right smack out in front of you and you come into him on a T-bone crash. Believe me, you haven't got a chance. In other words, *you* as a motorcycle rider *are morally responsible* for your own life.

Here's what to do under the condition one, above.

Always—*always*—ALWAYS—*ALWAYS* get your motorcycle down to such a speed that *you can stop it* or *swing in behind* the car, going down the street he came from. After all, a legal rate of speed is merely an average put out by law enforcement offices to govern your actions under ordinary conditions. The legal rate of speed for *you*, as a motorcycle rider, is any speed that you can control your vehicle under a given set of circumstances.

These days a chap with a scooter or a motorcycle has no difficulty finding an attractive girl companion, who is intrigued with the fascinating sport of motorcycling.

NOW FOR "ACCIDENT CONDITION" NUMBER TWO: That is where you, on your motorcycle are following a car, and getting ready to pass it. The car is going rather slowly when all of a sudden it swings to the left right in front of you (crash—you've had it). You see, *he* probably was looking for a street marker sign on the right side (they aren't very large), he finds it at the last moment and he turns across your lane of traffic. You were so close behind that you were in a blind spot in his mirror so he didn't even know you were there. A slightly different version accounts for the car coming toward you and turning in front of you. *In all cases* you assumed that he had seen you—*and he hasn't*. Remember, a motorcycle is a small vehicle.

KEEP THE THREE FOLLOWING SUGGESTIONS ALWAYS IN MIND:

1. Don't assume a stopped car at a boulevard stop sign sees you.

2. Don't pass a slow-moving car at an intersection.

3. Turn on your headlight one hour before the cars do.

A "Jack Rabbit" Club affair—and the rider lives up to the name.

"Body English" is used by experienced riders to help balance bike, as does this Triumph rider in a California desert event.

No, no, Fisby! Only when they're on the highway!

*The practiced desert enduro rider
knows that unexpected obstacles such
as this desert bush can produce a hazard.*

"Motor Cycling"

Beginner in rough country riding can scare himself with unexpected "wheelie" if full power applied suddenly. (Below)

Sliding around sharp bend at full power is called "ragged edge" riding. Done by expert Jim Hunter, it's key to fast cornering. (Bottom)

Through practice, and as time progresses, the new rider is apt to become overconfident which usually is not a good thing. The rider who respects his motorcycle and does not take chances and ride in a careless manner is certain to have a lot of pleasure from his bike. We urge every new rider to read the suggestions by many famous experts that appear in this book.

Keep Safety First— Common-sense Riding

Motorcycling is great fun and as safe as any method of transportation providing, of course, the rider is not reckless and uses ordinary good judgment. It is naturally important that the new rider, until he becomes familiar with his bike, keeps out of heavy traffic and practices in some street or road where there is a minimum of traffic.

Heading uphill on bumpy trail, rider's relaxed crouching position shows how some experts put weight on foot pegs instead of seat. (Top left)

Riding out a rugged desert trail, motorcyclist keeps throttle at steady setting, keeps weight on pegs instead of on seat over rough bumps. (Top right)

Weight on saddle rather than pegs can sometimes dump beginning rider on climb in rough terrain. (Below)

Experienced road rider shows complete control as he heels machine over to take fast bend. (Below)

Emerging from the cactus, expert demonstrates correct position with feet on pegs for safely executing a jump. (Opposite page)

Like auto seat belts, cycle helmets are useless if not worn. This rider's helmet is not only off his head but dangling dangerously from the handlebar. Passenger has good sense to keep helmet where it belongs: on his head. (Left)

Correct position for right hand. Throttle, front brake and hi-lo light switch are under control of these five fingers. (Below left)

Smart housewife knows that the right way to carry packages is in basket—not cradled in one arm or on handlebars. (Below center)

Looks unnerving but this is a perfectly safe maneuver in slow-moving city traffic. Rider remains in between-lanes space, doesn't jackrabbit. (Below right)

The safe and proper way to corner. (Bottom)

29

SAFE MOTORCYCLING—

"Safe Motorcycling" is reprinted in part through the courtesy of the Triumph Corporation, Towson, Baltimore 4, Maryland. The company provides the purchaser of each new Triumph with a booklet of the same title, based on the training given the London, England, metropolitan police motorcyclists.

IT IS NOT necessary to ride a motorcycle flat out to enjoy it. In fact, riding in an intelligent manner, and handling the motor as it should be handled, can provide as much enjoyment as pushing the bike to its limit—and in many cases, both bike and rider will be around longer as a result.

Many motorcycle accidents occur through the inability of the rider to stop his machine in time to avoid accident. When braking, do so while the motor is upright and on firm footing. Use both brakes—in conjunction with the gearbox. If braking must be carried out while the machine is being cornered, use the rear binder only. This rule also applies on slippery surfaces.

Choose the correct speed and gear to corner, and position the motorcycle on the right line before entering a bend. Don't enter a corner too fast, and don't accelerate through it. Instead, turn it on when coming out of the bend. Three questions the rider should ask when negotiating a curve

GO SLOW:—Especially in built up areas—crosswalks do not make ideal starting lines for impromptu drags. That guy lunging for safety is probably the traffic court judge our boy will have to face tomorrow.

are: "Am I on the right side of the road?" "Can I stay on the right side?" "Can I stop if some obstacle appears that is presently outside my field of vision?"

Concentration is an important ally of the motorcyclist. Concentration on a minor detail will often tip the rider off to something about to happen. Daydreaming, on the other hand, may result in an accident. Concentration will help insure the skillfull handling of the motorcycle, and cut down on missed shifts and hard braking.

Do not "tailboard" the vehicle ahead, but instead ride at a safe distance to the rear. The heady rider does this, and doesn't attempt to pass until the maneuver can be accomplished in perfect safety. Whenever in doubt—don't. Avoid those hairy flat-out runs past a car in third gear, while an approaching auto looms larger and larger and the margin of safety disappears.

When passing in the clear, however, don't linger next to the car being passed, while a quick check is made for possible good-looking females or other goodies aboard. Drive with deliberation and without hesitation.

At 60 m.p.h., a motorcycle travels 88 feet in one second. The average rider takes at least a second to find the brakes. Speed, therefore, should be used intelligently—and only in the right places. Anybody can ride fast enough to be dangerous.

Since many "Sunday" motorists develop a blind spot in regard to spotting approaching cycles, the bike horn should be used whenever necessary. Augment the hooter with hand and headlight signals, depending on the time of day. Signals are important—very few motorists possess psychic powers.

Lastly, it is wise to develop the art of courteous driving—something of a hard task when the rider has to cope with today's traffic conditions. The use of courtesy, plus the other recommendations listed, will make motorcycling more enjoyable for the motorcycle rider—and the other users of his particular stretch of highway.

CUTTING IN:—Just try this caper on a couple of taxis some time! Had the cyclist passed quickly instead of hesitating, those irate gentlemen would be beaming instead of steaming. Ride a bike in decisive fashion.

WHOA:—How to cup front tires in one easy lesson—anticipation of the stop light change would have enabled this rider to shut off half a block away.

CONCENTRATE:—On the road, not the scenery, that is! It doesn't take long for a bike to wander from the straight and narrow when the rider's mind is doing likewise.

REPRINTED from **CYCLE** "World's Largest Monthly Motorcycle Circulation"

Famous 4-cylinder overhead cam-shaft 500cc Gilera Grand Prix road racer. One of the world's fastest.

Opinions differ as to whether a two-stroke or four-stroke engine is the superior motorcycle power plant. Practically all of the large bikes have four-cycle engines and most of the lightweights are powered by two-cycle engines. There are advantages and disadvantages to each type of engine and for discussion as to the merits of each type we are including articles by two nationally known experts, Pete Colman and Jack McCormack, who are not only experienced motorcycle riders, but are connected with the sale of motorcycles.

THE "FOUR-CYCLE" MOTORCYCLE ENGINE
by Pete Colman
General Manager
BSA Motorcycles-Western, Member,
National Competition Committee
of the A.M.A.

Let's examine, for a moment, the term "four-cycle" or "four-stroke" as opposed to "two-cycle" or "two-stroke." Over the years, you have been most familiar with the conventional four-stroke design, perhaps without an awareness or knowledge of the basic difference between engine types.

The family automobile (with few exceptions) has always been powered with a four-cycle engine, as has the piston-type, propeller-driven aircraft and the inboard speed boat. On the other hand, your first introduction to two-cycle design might have been an outboard boat engine, or even a power mower . . . the type that required mixing oil with the gasoline. A few of today's modern two-stroke motorcycles are equipped with sep-

arate gasoline and oil tanks, the proper mixture of gas and oil obtained by means of an automatic oil injector.

In the early days of motorcycling, two-stroke engines and simple four-stroke engines were both used by pioneer manufacturers. With progress, as engineering and materials improved, the predominant motorcycle engine became that of four-stroke design. Not only in the United States, but throughout the world, manufacturers of motorcycles found their customers wanting more horsepower from larger-capacity powerplants. Through this evolution came the modern versions of overhead valve and overhead cam four-cycle engines.

The spark plugs of a four-cycle engine fire every other time that the piston reaches the top of the cylinder. This means the crankshaft or flywheel assembly makes two complete revolutions for every power impulse. These four-cycles are simple. As the piston goes downward, a raw gas and air mixture is drawn into the cylinder through the carburetor, manifold and the open inlet, or intake, valve, completing the "first cycle." The piston, reaching the bottom of the downward stroke, returns again to the top of the cylinder (with inlet and exhaust valves closed) and compresses the mixture of gas and air. Just as the piston nears the top of the cylinder, the spark plug triggers an explosion of the compressed gases, ending the "second cycle."

The explosion sends the piston downward again; this is the power stroke, or the "third cycle." As the piston starts to the top of the cylinder for the second time, the exhaust valve

The Harley-Davidson Sportster "V" twin is powerful, fast and world's second largest engine-capacity bike. (Left)

is open, and the burned gases are expelled past the valve and out the exhaust pipe. Thus the "fourth cycle," and two revolutions of the engine are completed.

True, the "four-stroke" has more working parts than a "two-stroke" engine. But these additional parts are an asset, not a liability . . . because in reality it means "more parts working" for performance and reliability. For example, all-round performance is more easily obtainable from four-cycle engines—good idling, smooth low-speed operation, and good top speed can be expected from a properly tuned four-stroke. Important, too, is the fact that the extra exhaust stroke of the four-stroke provides a cooling interlude that is not possible in the two-stroke system. Thus the four-stroke is normally less susceptible to overheating under trying conditions.

If a special-purpose engine is required, performance may be changed at will. Either excellent low-torque or superior top horsepower may be obtained by the fitting of various camshafts and special parts available. Even all-around performance may be improved with careful workmanship and tuning, if the hobbyist has a hankering to do so.

Maintenance of a four-cycle engine is comparable to a two-cycle. While more time is required for a complete overhaul, the four-cycle will operate for longer periods with less minor maintenance. The four-stroke is not prone to premature carbon formations in the combustion chamber, or exhaust system, or to oil-fouled spark plugs.

The "four-stroke" does not depend on any mixture of gas and oil for lubrication. All engine lubrication is accomplished through a central oil pump which separately directs oil to the crankshaft bearings, cylinder walls, valves and valve guides. The four-stroke rider may shut his throttle off on long downhill grades without fear of piston seizure, as piston lubrication does not depend on the gas-oil mixture.

Because of a wider power range, the four-stroke engine will accelerate quite nicely in high gear. On comparable engine sizes, the four-stroke develops more lugging power. Some standard production two-strokes are fitted with five-speed (and there's talk of a six-speed) gearboxes, fewer gear changes being required to keep the four-stroke within the usable power range. Here again, less maintenance is required on the four-stroke, but added gears will eventually require more maintenance.

Size for size, you may expect more miles per gallon of gas from the four-stroke engine. The two-stroke completes a power cycle every revolution of the engine, therefore using more gasoline. This does not mean that the two-stroke develops twice the power. Because it does fire each time the piston reaches the top of the stroke, and because of overlapping cycles, much of the volumetric efficiency is lost from each power stroke.

Factory engineering and race track development continues to keep pace with modern times, and tomorrow's four-cycle designs will far surpass today's modern developments. Yes, four-cycle internal combustion engines have a true place in motorcycles . . . and a long bright future!

THROTTLE
CONTROL
WIRE

THROTTLE

AIR INTAKE

JET

FLOAT

Diagram of a conventional two-stroke (two-cycle means the same design).

Spanish Montesa is a popular and fast two-stroke lightweight with a unique starter pedal and long gearshift lever. (Below)

THE "TWO-CYCLE" MOTORCYCLE ENGINE
by Jack McCormack
Vice-President and General Manager, U.S. Suzuki Corporation

Is Detroit all wrong? If not, why is the two-stroke engine found in the great majority of lightweight motorcycles today? Certainly Detroit is not wrong. But remember they produce large capacity engines, most of which are either six- or eight-cylinder designs.

When we speak of lightweight motorcycles we are speaking of engine displacements that range from 50 cubic centimeters to 250 cubic centimeters and of no more than two cylinders, with the predominance being single-cylinder types.

Consider that the two-stroke engine fires every revolution rather than every other revolution as in the four-stroke designs. Thus, two-stroke engine manufacturers are able to achieve a smooth power flow in engines of twin- or single-cylinder design, while this smoothness is obtainable in a four-stroke design only by employing the use of multiple cylinders firing alternately. This type engine is expensive to produce.

Thus, it is generally conceded in displacements of 250 cc or under that the two-stroke engine offers many advantages, while above these displacements the four-stroke begins to become more practical. This is not only for the reasons previously mentioned, but for reasons such as the fact that the modern two-stroke engine has only

An overhead-camshaft British Norton Racer.

three basic moving parts: two are reciprocating while one is rotating. Therefore, it does not absorb a great deal of the energy developed in order to move its own parts, while the four-stroke engine has many reciprocating parts that drain the engine of much of its own energy. However, as engine displacement increases, the four-stroke gradually absorbs this loss and makes up for it in increased volumetric efficiency.

Although the two-stroke design has been with us for many years, it has really just begun to come into its own. The recent rapid developments of this type engine have startled the internal combustion engine world. The power-per-cubic-inch increases in four-stroke engines have, in the last decade, been less sensational. Furthermore, the increases shown have been primarily the product of ever-increasing mechanical complexities and/ or exotic fuels. In contrast, the two-stroke designs have made quite amazing progress in efficiency, while retaining their basic mechanical simplicity. There is no evidence that the end is yet in sight. As it stands now, in the 250cc and smaller displacement classes, the modern two-stroke can line up alongside the four-stroke in vying for consumer acceptance, standing on its own merits, and come out on top often as not.

In the following paragraphs we will analyze both types and let you evaluate their merits for yourself.

In order to simplify the comparisons in construction, maintenance and repair, we will stick with single-cylinder types. There are six major components in the two-stroke design, three of

these are stationary; the crankcase, cylinder, and cylinder head. The crankshaft, connecting rod, and piston are, of course, the moving components.

In a typical pushrod-type overhead valve four-stroke you will find besides the same stationary items the following additional paraphernalia: Two valves with guides, four valve springs with keepers and collars, two pushrods, two rockers with shafts, two tappets with guides, two cams with necessary driving gear, two oil pumps and a separate oil tank with necessary plumbing.

At periodic low-mileage intervals you will find that a four-stroke requires tappet adjustment in order to maintain normal engine performance and also protect the valve seats. Skill and knowledge are required here and one normally entrusts this task to a skilled mechanic.

With additional mileage it will be necessary to remove carbon and re-seat the valves. Later the valves will need replacement as they become burned, worn and warped, likewise the guides and springs call for attention. At this time it is advisable to replace piston rings or face the problem of "blow-by." This all usually requires the service of a professional mechanic.

Of course, the two-stroke does not suffer from expenses imposed on the four-stroke by valve gear. However, you will find carbon formations somewhat more of a problem in the engine and exhaust systems than in four-strokes. This problem will vary, however, depending much on the use of the vehicle. If it is used for short, low-speed trips, the engine would require decoking to remove carbon deposits at low-mileage intervals.

Although if there are at least occasional lengthy rides at reasonably fast speeds, the engine and exhaust systems will rid themselves of much excessive carbon.

When it does become necessary to remove excessive carbon deposits, it is a relatively simple and quick job that the owner can accomplish himself with the tools furnished in the tool kit of each new machine. Because it requires little special knowledge or mechanical aptitude, most owners can and do accomplish this job on their own. Should poor compression indicate the need for new piston rings, it is a very simple operation to lift the cylinder and replace the rings.

One area where both types are quite similar in relation to repair is the crankcase. When dismantling for bearing service, it is a job for an experienced mechanic with the necessary tools and equipment. The two-stroke does not have the valve gear and oil pumps to contend with. However, they do require precise refitting so that the cases are properly sealed, as the fuel charge is initially compressed in the crankcase.

As mentioned earlier, the two-stroke has a power stroke to every revolution while the four-stroke has one only with every other revolution, thus giving the two-stroke the equivalent of multi-cylinder smoothness. However, it does not mean that the two-stroke will develop twice the horse-power of a comparable four-stroke. This is not possible due to the relatively short duration of both intake and exhaust strokes. The periods of time available for these functions are approximately half that provided in a four-stroke design,

although duration of compression and power strokes compare more favorably with the four-stroke.

Other loss of efficiency stems from dilution of the fresh charge with burned gases remaining from the previous combustion cycle, also a small percentage of the fresh charge will possibly be lost through the exhaust port.

This really means that the volumetric efficiency of the two-stroke is less than that of the four-stroke, thus causing some loss of the advantage gained by firing once every revolution. However, the well-designed two-stroke retains a great deal of this advantage, at the same time imposing less stress on bearing surfaces.

Sometimes when listening to a two-stroke exhaust note, it sounds as if they are really very high-revving units, but remember they are firing twice as often as the four-stroke. Thus a two-stroke at 5,000 rpm would sound like a four-stroke at 10,000 rpm. A multi-cylinder two-stroke, such as Suzuki's Grand Prix four-cylinder 250 is really singing when it's at work.

Two-strokes used to be known for their erratic idling and irregular firing at low speeds. But through the years, research has been able to virtually eliminate these characteristics in today's better designs. A modern two-stroke engine immediately settles down to even firing when placed under load and is outstandingly smooth through the full range of operation.

Four-stroke engines never have suffered from erratic idling unless they were modified for competition or just out of tune. However, neither do they offer the smoothness of operation in a relatively small displacement engine.

The usual method of lubricating the two-stroke engine is by mixing oil with the gasoline, although at least two major companies are now offering oil injected from a separate reservoir. In this system the difference is that the oil is injected into the intake port rather than being introduced in a mixture. From this point on, the system does not differ. The gasoline with oil, or with oil injected, as the case may be, is drawn into the crankcase where most of the oil is separated due to the centrifugal action of the flywheels. This clean oil collects in drops on the walls of the crankcase, drains into pockets provided, and is then channeled to the big end bearing. The remaining oil is held in suspension and distributed to the cylinder walls and piston in the form of a mist.

This may appear to be a rather haphazard method when you compare it with the typical four-stroke lubricating system, where oil is delivered to the various areas under pressure and in pre-determined quantities. Regardless, the fuel/oil system works, and quite well at that. Especially when you consider that it is always fresh clean oil and not recirculated old oil as in the four-stroke. The four-stroke system of "controlled flow" has advantages in that it allows full lubrication of engine parts without overloading the engine with excess oil because the excess oil is picked up by scavenger pumps and returned to the reservoir. These systems are recirculating types and thus end up recirculating abrasives and acids that are natural by-products of engine operation. If a rider fails to change his oil at the prescribed intervals, clean his oil tank, filter and screen, the eventual destruction of his engine is accelerated.

Sometimes with a two-stroke engine excess smoke from the exhaust will be noted when the motor is first started. This is caused from oil dripping from the hot interior surface into the crankcase area after the engine has set awhile. On restarting it is flung by the flywheels into the transfer passages, and until the excess is disposed of, you will see excessive smoke through the exhaust. Although sometimes annoying, it does offer certain advantages in that your engine is receiving extra lubrication during a critical period.

Usually the two-stroke will consume about 15 per cent more gasoline than the four-stroke due

Canadian Mike Duff racing in England.

Yamaha road racing riders Tony Murphy (left) and Al Gunter, holder of many national championship titles, are shown with Yamaha factory mechanics at National Motorcycle Rally in Dodge City, Kansas.

to the number of firing strokes and its somewhat lesser volumetric efficiency. Oil consumption, however, is about the same as a four-stroke in that you do not have periodic expenses of oil change.

In operating procedures there is little difference. Although the two-stroke rider has no worries about valve-float, he does have one problem peculiar to the two-stroke. When coasting down long grades he must remember to allow some throttle opening to insure lubrication, for if he closes it he is also shutting off his oil supply to the engine. This is not true on the injection type unit as they will continue to inject even with the throttle closed.

Regardless of what type engine you eventually choose, it is wise to remember that the proper care and feeding will earn you years of fun and enjoyment with little in the way of mechanical trouble to spoil your pleasure.

In the next three sections many different makes and models of motorcycles are illustrated and described. It is impossible to list every model and every make of motorcycle available to the United States buyer as new models are introduced and some models discontinued as the months and years go by.

This information should enable the new buyer to make a decision as to what make and model is best suited for his specific use. Usually the lighter weight bikes are popular with the beginner. It has been the history of motorcycling that often the man who purchases a lightweight bike soon steps up to a heavier one with more power and speed. It should be remembered that many states do not allow the extremely small lightweights on freeways or turnpikes and this is as it should be.

Some states have a five-horsepower minimum requirement before any make is allowed on a high-speed road; however, we feel that the speed of the cycle is more important than the horsepower and certainly no bike with a speed of less than 70 miles per hour is suitable for high-speed traffic on freeways and turnpikes.

MUSTANG *"Thoroughbred" (United States)*

19.4 cu. in./Four-cycle, 4-speed transmission, left side shift. A rugged machine by America's pioneer in the lightweight field. Swinging-arm rear suspension, heavy-duty shocks, telescopic front forks, 12.5 h.p. 2.4-gal. gas tank for 155-175 mile range; 2-qt. oil capacity. Wheelbase: 53 in. Overall length: 75½ in. Total height: 41 in. Seat height: 28½ in. Max. width (handlebars): 28½ in. Tires: 4.00 x 12, 2-ply. All Mustang models—trail or street—feature liberal use of well-chromed parts including related wheels, kickstarter, flywheel, part of tank, hubs, etc. Magneto-generator electrics, with all lights conforming to all state laws.

MUSTANG *"Delivercycle" (United States)*
319cc/Four-cycle. Four-speed gearbox, left side shift. A specialized machine of 3-wheeler design, capable of churning out 12½ h.p. at 3,600 rpm. Gas mileage is about 50 mpg. This handy machine is popular in large cities for local and across-town deliveries of up to 300 lb. It is popular with a wide range of service shops, parts suppliers and commercial firms because of its low operating and driver costs, and its reliability in meeting delivery deadlines.

DUCATI *"Sport 80"* (Italy)
80cc/Two-cycle/Single cylinder/
Unit construction. Three-speed
transmission, left handlebar shift
in unit with clutch 125 lbs. A sporty
gadabout, thoroughly practical for
large campuses or companies where
commuting between classes or
factory buildings and warehouses
is of some distance. Large toolbox
under seat provides handy storage.
Frame is double loop; long-stroke
forks are also of sturdy
construction.

HONDA 50 CA-100 (CA-102
w/electric starter) (Japan)
49cc/Four-cycle/Single cylinder.
Three-speed gearbox, left side shift.
140 lbs. (155 lbs. w/electric starter).
The little bear that got the ball
rolling. Ultra-easy for anyone to ride,
with automatic clutch. Mileage
figures up to 200 mpg give upper
economy under proper conditions.
Will carry passenger in comfort if
not speed. May be ridden with skirts;
plastic leg shields protect against
wind, dirt, road oil. A well-built
leader in the Honda line-up.

YAMAHA *"Rotary Jet 80"* YGI
(Japan)
80cc/Two-cycle/Single cylinder/
Unit construction. Four-speed gearbox, left side shift. 140 lbs.
Monocoque steel construction for
light weight and long-on-torque
power makes a real performer.
Mileage is 170-plus mpg. Long, dual
saddle is optional with short seat
and pack-rack. A particularly fine
bike for beginners, with enough oats
and agility to satisfy the expert.

YAMAHA *"Riverside 55"* YJ-1.
(Japan)
55cc/Two-cycle/Single cylinder/
Unit construction. Three-speed gearbox, left side shift. 140 lbs.
Monocoque steel frame and front
forks with integral rear fender hold
weight without sacrificing; indeed
strengthens rigidity. Pleasing tank
design is functional with large knee
pads at sides. Over 200 mpg
economy.

HODAKA *"Ace"-90* (Japan)
90cc/two-cycle. Four-speed gearbox,
left side shift. 155 lbs. A superb
lightweight for road or trail.
American thinking combined with
Japanese production. Double loop
frame, alloy brakes, folding pegs,
giant 2½-gallon tank, big saddle,
large headlamp, ball-end levers, high
8-inch clearance, aircraft bolts and
locknuts. High chainguard permits
various optional rear sprockets.
Chain guide incorporated. Washable
air filter.

SUZUKI K15. (Japan)
80cc/Two-cycle/Single cylinder/
Unit construction. Four-speed transmission, left side shift. 154 lbs. A
fine trailing and hunting mount with
all the usual features and some well
thought-out extras. Broad seat is well
contoured, pleated and of nonskid
finish to hold driver in saddle.
Engine-protecting skid plate comes
well up, and down tube bracket is
added for reinforcement. Knobby
tires are of coarsest pattern for trac-
tion in deep sand, mud, pebbly
streams. Dual sprockets are provided
for changeover in short order.

HONDA 90 CA-200 (Japan)
86.7cc/Four-cycle/Single cylinder.
Four-speed gearbox, left side shift.
188 lbs. In style and tradition of
Honda's 50cc Super Sport, but with
more beans (6½ h.p.) and other

refinements. A logical step up for
those who prefer the size of the 50's
but need greater power. Numerous
accessories are available to give more
of a sports flavor without loss of
function or reliability.

**YAMAHA "Omaha Trailmaster 80"
MGI-T (Japan)**
80cc/Two-cycle/Single cylinder/
Unit construction. Three-speed
transmission, left side shift or
automatic clutch. 135 lbs. Bigger

brother of the Omaha Trail 55
MJ2-T, the 80 gives greater speeds
and flexibility as well as climbing
power, especially at higher altitudes.
Skid plate and high fender, pack-
rack, and full lighting are standard.

**YAMAHA "Trailmaster" YGI-T
(Japan)**
80cc/Two-cycle/Single cylinder/
Unit construction. Four-speed gearbox, left side shift. 140 lbs. All
features of the Street 80, with added
goodies such as oversize rear
sprocket, guard plate for engine,

abbreviated front fender, knobby
tires, higher "Western" bars, etc. A
"packer's delight" for hauling gear
into the back country, the "Trailmaster" has also done distinguished
work in lightweight-class racing
events.

HONDA "Trail 55" (Japan)
55cc/Four-cycle/Single cylinder/
Unit construction. Three-speed transmission, automatic clutch. 140 lbs.
Individual styling with large diameter,
single-tube frame and pressed steel

forks. Has brake controls in two
spots, foot and grip, for maximum
control in cobbly country. Quick-
change sprockets convert gearing to
needs. Knobbed tires and lighting
are standard features.

CAPRIOLO "Antelope" (Italy)
75cc/Four-cycle/Single cylinder/
Unit construction/Overhead cam.
Four-speed gearbox, right side shift.
160 lbs. Small displacement with
"big-bike" features. Sports styling
and performance with OHC, all-alloy

engine. 160 mpg economy. Strong
pressed-steel frame with an appearance of tube construction. Also
available in 100cc "Gazelle" and
125cc "Cheetah." Conversion kits
available to turn street jobs into
mountain climbers quickly.

DUCATI "Mountaineer 90" (Italy)
86cc/Two-cycle/Single cylinder/
Unit construction. Three-speed
gearbox, left handgrip shift w/clutch
release. 150 lbs. Light weight and
sturdy construction blend with
pleasing styling. Feature of hand

shift on clutch control enables gear
changing while balancing with both
feet. Fan-cooled engine fights
overheating even while stopped
or picking through arduous terrain.
Engine-transmission drive is by gears.

JAWA *"Trials Scrambler"*
(Czechoslovakia)
*125cc/Four-cycle/Single cylinder/
Four-speed gearbox. Unit construction. Smallest in capacity of the four
available Jawa trials machines is this
125cc model. (175cc, 250cc and*
*350cc machines complete the trials
series.) Simplicity of design and
rugged reliability have been the
keynote of this big-league European
motorcycle builder for many years
and no change has been made in
that basic policy.*

HONDA *"Benly" Touring CA-95
(Japan)*
*150cc/Four-cycle/Twin cylinder/
Overhead cams. Four-speed gearbox,
left side shift. 246 lbs. With 16½ hp,
the Benly qualifies for most freeways
and turnpikes, usually with a*
*minimum of 15. Has feel of a full-
size machine, yet economy is substantial with near 130 mpg tallies.
Engine has all features of larger
displacement model, including compact valve train with overhead
camshafts.*

BULTACO *"Mercurio" (Spain)*
*175cc/Two-cycle/Single cylinder.
Four-speed gearbox, right-hand shift.
200 lbs. Although not a road racer
like its big brother the "Metralla,"
Bultaco's "Mercurio" has benefited
from the big bike's experiences.*
*Basically, it is a sturdy, man-size
machine that puts out 18 hp without
fuss, and has a nicely stable low
center of gravity. Other assets include
17-in. wheels and very smooth
handling for either city stop-and-go
and parking, or for tooling down
the pike.*

BULTACO *"Motocross" and
"Motocross Scrambler" (Spain)*
*246cc/Two-cycle/Single cylinder.
Unit construction. Four-speed gearbox, right side shift. 209 lbs. While
the "Scrambler" version differs in
some details from the basic "Moto-
cross," the following covers major
points of both: 12.1 compression
ratio, with Spanish Amal 30mm
carburetion. A rugged all-metal,
11-plate clutch transfers power to
constant mesh (1 down, 3 up) gearbox. Ground clearance is 10 in. for a*
*54 in. wheelbase and a seat height
of 31¼ in. Primary and final drives
are via single row chains. The
Rickman frame has been designed to
take anything a 500cc mill can put
out. Gas tank, fenders, saddle and
side fairings and the air cleaner are
all of high-strength Fiberglass molded
in England by Avon. Gearbox, the
manufacturers say, has all shafts on
ball bearings and can take a full
100 hp load. Beside these two models,
a further variant is available: the
36 hp T. T. Scrambler.*

HONDA *CB-160 (Japan)*
*A 160cc, OHC twin-cylinder
machine, the Honda CB-160
develops 16.5 BHP @ 10,000 RPM;
offers buyers the only crankshaft in
its class supported by four main
heavy-duty bearings.
Other features include push-button
electric starting, an extra-large
capacity battery, precision ram-
tuned carburetors and special*
*telescopic front suspension.
Styled after the famous Honda
factory racers, the Honda CB-160
is a tubular frame, "competition-
type" machine, designed to provide
lightweight smoothness, yet with the
performance of heavier models.
Top speed for the 282-pound
Honda CB-160 is estimated at
75 mph; fuel consumption at
116 mpg.*

Montesa *"Impala-cross" (Spain)*
175cc/Two-cycle/Single cylinder/
Unit construction. Four-speed gear-
box, right side shift. 218 lbs. VIVA!
The little machine with the
Napoleonic complex fails to realize,
much less admit, that it's not a "big
job." For the occasional racer or

would-be-thought-of-as competitor,
features and styling not only give
the message, but do the job. Quick-
fill cap on big tank for long trips;
narrow racing bars and alloy rims
with choice of tire patterns are plus
features.

Honda *"Hawk" CB-72 and*
"Superhawk" CB-77 (Japan)
250cc and 305cc/4-cycle/Twin
cylinder/Overhead cam/Dual carbs.
Four-speed gearbox, left side shift.
300 lbs. A strong appeal is made to
the sportsman and the sports-minded
by the Hawk series machines. Docile
enough for daily street usage, they

possess capabilities for week-end
racing on the road circuits or may be
tuned for pure competition. Acces-
sories from the factory enable the
owner to convert to any desired
extent, enhancing the sporting
aspect. Electric starter, tachometer
are standard.

Triumph *"Mountain Cub" T20SM*
(England)
200cc/Four-cycle/Single cylinder/
Unit construction. Four-speed gear-
box, right side shift. 210 lbs. All the
speed, handling and "feel" of a big
motorcycle are joined in this light-
weight which takes a backseat to

none. High clearance with long-
stroke suspension front and rear,
large diameter wheels and high
exhaust give go-anywhere capacity.
Engine proven in competition,
constantly developed. Available in
strictly street trim (Model T20).

Bultaco *"Matador" (Spain)*
200cc/Two-cycle-Single cylinder/
Unit construction. Four-speed gear-
box, right side shift. 209 lbs. A truly
all-round scooter that lends itself to
every application. With polished
cases on current models. 20-hp

rating. Close ratio gears on first three
with wide jump to fourth; ideal for
trailing with usable highway speed.
High ground clearance and dyno-
tuned exhaust muffler. Shocks have
long travel and five-way adjustment.
Front forks have five-inch travel.

Valiant *"Sportsman" (United States)*
200cc/Two-cycle/Single cylinder.
Four-speed gearbox. 51-in. wheel-
base. 200 lbs. This is the big brother
of the Valiant "Compact" and is
equally intended for street or trail
use. Features include telescopic
forks, swinging arm suspension,
luggage carrier under buddy seat.

Engine is the famous Villiers 200cc,
fed from a 2½-gal. tank with ½-gal.
reserve. Horsepower restrictors are
available for junior license holders.
All models are fully equipped with
road lights, speedometer, horn and
passenger foot pegs. Wheel bearings
are Timken with flange separators
for quick tire removal.

Harley-Davidson *"Scat" BTH*
(United States)
175cc/Two-cycle/Single cylinder/
Unit construction. Three-speed trans-
mission, left side shift. 220 lbs.
Just the trick for trail-time with
huge overlay sprocket, low first and
second gears with high third for road

cruising. Available options include
alloy rims (shown) and Hunting and
Fishing kit; knobbed tires, gearing,
etc. Extremely rugged construction,
sturdy controls, folding pegs. High
front fender is of self-cleaning design
for thick mud, weeds.

BSA "Starfire Trial-Cat" 615-T, "Enduro Star" B40-ES (England) 250cc, 350cc/Four-cycle/Single cylinder/Unit construction. Four-speed gearbox, right side shift. 264 lbs., 290 lbs. Equipped with lighting, muffler and knobby tires, both models (virtually identical in appearance) make excellent mounts for the man or family who must suffice on one machine for both road and trail riding. Gearbox uses wide ratios for best results in rough country. Quick-change rear sprocket allows switchover for usages in minutes. Low compression and cams designed for lugging keep operating temperatures low.

HARLEY-DAVIDSON "Sprint H" H (United States) 250cc/Four-cycle/Single cylinder/Unit construction. Four-speed gearbox, right side shift. 271 lbs. For trailing and roadwork, a bike incorporating Italian design and craftsmanship with American parts and know-how. With pass-through exhaust and abbreviated front fender, small "scrambles" tank, and oversize cartridge air cleaner, it's set for the sod. In street trim as the Sprint C, with low muffler, four-gallon gas tank, big front fender, and direct-mounting cleaner.

MONTESA "Impala Sport" (Spain) 175cc/Two-cycle/Single cylinder/Unit construction. Four-speed gearbox, right side shift. 218 lbs. VIVA! The little machine with the Napoleonic complex fails to realize, much less admit that it's not a "big job." For the occasional racer or would-be-thought-of-as competitor, features and styling not only give the message, but do the job. Quick-fill cap on big tank for long trips; narrow racing bars and alloy rims with choice of tire patterns are plus features.

BMW R27 (Germany) 250cc/Four-cycle/Single cylinder/Unit construction. Four-speed transmission, left side shift, shaft rear drive. 345 lbs. An extremely dependable, low-maintenance, high-torque single with all the plus features of the popular BMW twins. Has Earles-type front forks, side-straddle kick starter. Very popular with messengers because of dependability, economy, easy starting, and good lugging ability.

BSA "B40 Sportsman" (England) 350cc/Four-cycle/Single cylinder/Unit construction. Four-speed gearbox, right side shift. 299 lbs. A zesty performer, combining light weight with jazzed engine. High compression, racing camshaft, big-bore carburetor with rugged connecting rod and roller bearing lower end mean lots of go with little down-time. Sharp looks combine blue paint and chrome/alloy accents.

PARILLA "Tourist" (Italy) 250cc/Four-cycle/Single cylinder/Unit construction. Four-speed gearbox, right side shift. 245 lbs. The road version, in sports trim, of the highly competitive and most successful 250cc "Wildcat," and the road racing "Grand Sport Race." The same engine-head and cams being changed to allow normal street usage. Power/weight ratio is superb, making a thrilling mount for the most demanding.

BULTACO *"Metralla" 62-RS (Spain)*
*200cc/Two-cycle/Single cylinder/
Unit construction. Four-speed gearbox, right side shift. 213 lbs. A true
sporting machine, featuring the TSS
racing engine in a street chassis.
Large, scooped front brake, alloy*

*rims, 29mm Dell'Orto carb with
remote float, dyno-tuned exhaust,
low clip-on bars, racing chain and
sprockets, all-suede adjustable racing
saddle. Big tank has quick-fill cap.
Output rated at 30-31 hp.*

TRAIL-BREAKER *(United States)
134cc/Two-cycle/Single cylinder.
(West Bend) Three-speed transmission, left side hand shift. Fluid
coupling. 193 lbs. Revolutionary two-
wheel drive via shaft through frame,
U-jointed, to chain-drive miter boxes.
Solid suspension with flexible two-ply*

*tires of 6.70x15 size. Wheels store
extra fuel or water. Very light despite
"earth-mover" appearance. Front
package tray, rear saddle (as shown)
optional. Extremely high clearance
with fold-up footrests. Climbs
steepest inclines.*

PARILLA *"Wildcat Scrambler" (Italy)
125cc/Four-cycle/Single cylinder/
Unit construction. Four-speed gearbox, right side shift. 194 lbs. A
machine that inspires devotion from
the most blase, it has beauty as well
as performance. Dual sprocket setup*

*for quick changes in role from high-
way to byway. Full lighting and road
equipment are provided, all of which
are easily stripped if a call to battle is
heard. Good handling is inherent in a
well-planned, dual or (triple, if you
please) motorcycle.*

HONDA *"Scrambler" CL-72 (Japan)
250cc/Four-cycle/Twin cylinder/
Overhead cams/Dual carbs. Four-
speed gearbox, left side shift. 315 lbs.
Deemed by many to be the ideal
dual-purpose bike for street and
scrambling or cow-trailing. Very
agile and maneuverable, with firm*

*suspension. Sporting appearance fol-
lows function. Manual starter, with
both tachometer and speedometer.
Frame has front down-tube with two-
tube cradle under engine and skid
plate. Sturdy rims aid in off-the-road
longevity.*

HONDA *"Dream" Touring CA-77
(Japan)
305cc/Four-cycle/Twin cylinder/
Overhead cams. Four-speed gearbox,
left side shift. 355 lbs. For the road-
riding enthusiast, the top of the*

*Honda models offers comfort,
economy, and wide fenders to protect
its owner in inclement weather.
Mileage is approximately 70 mpg.
Rated horsepower is 25. Comes
standard with electric starter.*

YAMAHA *"Santa Barbara 125" YA-6
(Japan)
123cc/Two-cycle/Single cylinder/
Unit construction. Four-speed gearbox, left side shift. 242 lbs. A nice
single for those who detest kicking
is equipped with electric starter.*

*Latest model has oil-injection unit.
Rear chain fully enclosed for cleanli-
ness and safety. Long, dual saddle
optional. Finish is typical of marque:
flawless. Details are also exquisite
and fully functional.*

YAMAHA *"Catalina Sports"* YDS-3 (Japan)
250cc/Two-cycle/Twin cylinders/ Unit construction. Five-speed gearbox, left side shift. 340 lbs. A true sporting machine with all the flavor and many features of a road racer. Dual exhausts have removable muffler inserts; tachometer/speedo combination is provided; large alloy hubs and brakes are standard. Dual carburetion with oil injection (Yamaha's Autolube) provides power and dependability in an enjoyable touring/sports cycle.

JAWA *"250," "350"* (Czechoslovakia)
248cc, 344cc/2-cycle/Single cylinder unit construction. Four-speed gearbox, left side shift. 283 lbs., 302 lbs. A most respected family of motorcycles; winners of many honors in trials, touring, and racing. Unique rectangular tubing frame, extra-long travel forks. Ride is unparalleled for comfort. A big bike in size, but extremely economical. Large displacement provides more adequate power for most riders.

COTTON *"Trials Special"* (England)
250cc/Two-cycle/Single cylinder/ Unit construction. Four-speed gearbox, right side shift. Torsion front suspension, well-braced tubular frame, optional 2¾-gallon tank and reliable Villiers 32A engine/trans unit with gear spacing ideal for trials or trails make a top-category backcountry bike. Has chrome steel fenders and exhaust-muffler setup. May be fitted with lights quite easily.

NORTON *"Electa 400"* (England)
397cc/Four-cycle/Twin cylinder/ Unit construction. Four-speed gearbox, right side shift. 425 lbs. (estimated). Features electric starter in alloy engine with separate cams forward and aft of parallel cylinders. One-piece crankshaft has center flywheel, ball and roller bearings. Frame is most unique, with air foil-shape down tube, bolt-on aft section of two-loop design to hold gas tank, mount swing arm and cradle engine. Uses big alloy hubs, brakes as on 750cc models.

BSA *"Royal Star"* (England)
500cc/650cc/Four-cycle/Twin cylinders/Unit construction. Four-speed gearbox, right side shift. 385, 390 lbs. A highway cruiser in two popular displacement categories. Identification is by metallic blue paint on 30-cubic-inch model and candy-apple red on 40-incher. Touring cams, single 1⅛-inch Amal carb combine with 9:1 compression to give good power and low speed characteristics (one-inch carb on 500cc). Soft, adjustable ride and wide comfortable saddle for one or two.

BMW *R50, R60* (Germany)
500cc, 600cc/Four-cycle/Twin cylinder/Unit construction. Four-speed gearbox, left side shift, shaft rear drive. 425, 430 lbs. Deemed by many discriminating road riders as the epitome in motorcycles, their advocates are legion and chauvinistic. Very smooth, quiet, and clean. Earles-type front forks and horizontally opposed cylinder layout make them a special breed of cat, but rare shaft drive contributes most to attributes.

MATCHLESS "Apache" G12CS (England)
650cc/Four-cycle/Twin cylinders. Four-speed transmission, right side shift. Dual purpose mount, popular for many years on the west coast. Smooth operation and outstanding suspension make "Apache" a winner for cow-trailing, prospecting, rock-hounding; capable of being ridden to the wilds, in, and back. All alloy engine, notably strong, smooth clutch and transmission. Alloy fenders and sports tank standard. Also available in street trim with suitable tires and large, touring tank. Outstandingly smooth engine.

NORTON "Atlas" (England)
750cc/Four-cycle/Twin cylinder/ Dual carbs. Four-speed gearbox, right side shift, 420 lbs. Double loop "Featherbed" frame and "Road-holder" forks combine to make the Atlas an extremely comfortable roadster. Chrome steel fenders, contemporary sculptured tank, and ultra-fine detailed finish give top-drawer appeal. Power range is broad and smooth, good flexibility in all gears.

VELOCETTE "Venom Clubman" (England)
500cc/Four-cycle/Single cylinder. Four-speed gearbox, right side shift. 350 lbs. (approximately). Not mass-produced by current standards, the Velo is popular with mechanics, enthusiasts who appreciate its near hand-built perfection. An old-line company with sound experience in the racing field and the courage to adapt these developments to road machinery, Velocette puts out a soundly evolutionary machine with solid horsepower and agility in handling.

ROYAL ENFIELD "Interceptor" (England)
750cc/Four-cycle/Twin cylinders/ Dual carbs. Four-speed gearbox, right side shift. 414 lbs. Big displacement twin from England has long (57-inch) wheelbase for good roadability, sta-bility. Engine is physically large, in single loop frame. Horsepower is rated 58 at 6700 rpm, using two 1-3/16-inch Monobloc carburetors, magneto ignition. RE Interceptors in racing trim hold records on tracks and at drag strips.

TRIUMPH "Sports Tiger" T100SC (England)
500cc/Four-cycle/Twin cylinder/ Unit construction. Four-speed gearbox, right side shift. 335 lbs. A dual-purpose bike for street or trail, easily converted to a gusty racing bike. Ideal for cow-trailing with good power, high, single pipe. Comes with light, alloy sports fenders, small head-lamp, and direct a-c lighting and magneto for elimination of battery. Other specs similar to Speed Tiger.

BSA "Lightning Rocket" A65-21 (England)
650cc/Four-cycle/Twin cylinder/ Unit construction. Four-speed gearbox, right side shift. 390 lbs. Hot new streetster features dual carburetion and ignition, full race cams, high-alloy steel gears, high-compression aluminum pistons, and comes standard with tach and speedo. Highly chromed and polished with welcome no-leak engine/transmission unit. Notably quiet in operation. Firm to soft ride for road comfort. Lightweight front brake. An extremely highspeed bike with strong torque all the way.

650cc PANTHER. It's a 650cc single cylinder machine employing magneto ignition and D.C. generator for lighting. Based on the former 600cc version, the latest model puts out its maximum horsepower at 5300 rpm. The clutch has been improved by the use of hard fabric clutch blocks in place of the old cork clutch. Now the front chain can run in a grease mixture, rather than light oil which tended to leak.

Throughout the years V-type engine design has been prevalent in United States motorcycle engineering. With few exceptions the most popular motorcycle engines produced in America have been of V design, such as Harley-Davidson, Indian, Excelsior, Thor, Pope, Merkel, and practically all the others. Occasionally some U. S. engineer would offer different designs, such as when Harley-Davidson twice built an opposed twin—first, in 1919, and later an opposed twin mounted transversely in the frame, for the U. S. Army. Indian also built a transverse opposed twin, and also a small Model "O" opposed twin in 1917.

The popularity of the V-twin in America, and probably the reason that this design still prevails, is the fact that all U. S. cars with 8-cylinder engines are of V design, and about 90% of the cars now built in this country have V-type engines.

Two largest displacement motorcycles manufactured in the world are Harley-Davidsons, the largest being the 74 OHV Twin. The other is the 55 cu. in. Sportster.

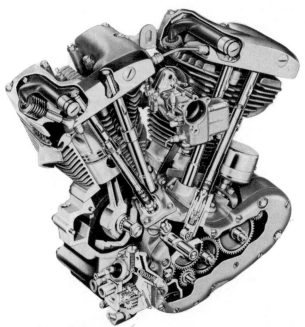

17th-CENTURY COSTUME MAKES UNUSUAL SCOOTER SUIT
A 20th-century scooterist dressed in 17th-century garb, with a tricorner hat instead of a helmet, was recently seen at the Allesley, Coventry factory of Triumph Engineering Ltd! He was Mr. Alfred Howard of Lambeth, London's only town crier and twice champion of the 28 town criers in England, who was visiting the company's Service Department. Under the sponsorship of the British Board of Trade and the British Travel Association, Mr. Howard has toured some 14 countries to publicize holidays in Britain. As well as for personal transport, he uses this Triumph Tina scooter for much of his procession work.

For over half a century the largest motorcycle show in the world takes place in London, England each year. Motorcycles are exhibited from almost every motorcycle producing country. Shown here are many of the models in the recent show. Many of them are sold overseas and have features that sometimes differ from the same makes sold in the United States, for instance, short stubby handlebars, license plate brackets mounted on the front fender and saddles. Most cycles imported for sale in the United States have equipment to comply with laws of our various states. Head and tail lights, handlebars, gearing, tires, rear-view mirrors (a California law requirement), color and chrome combinations and other differences are usually installed at the respective factories before shipment. Of course, here in the States we use tires, not "tyres," and color instead of "colour."

Shown here are many new models and makes displayed at the London Motorcycle Show. For over 50 years this show (now held in Earl's Court, London) has been the largest motorcycle show in the world with exhibits from every cycle producing country. Many of the makes shown, however, differ from the models sold in the United States. Usually handlebars, head and tail lights, direction signals, colors and chrome combinations are different.

This wise young Tina rider has "Gayplas" rear view mirrors fitted to her automatic scooter so that she is fully aware of traffic movements behind her. The "Gayplas" fairing gives her good weather protection. Both are products of Motoplas and are available in a variety of colors to match the scooter. (Left)

The 200cc Ariel Arrow, introduced to offset the problem of high insurance costs, is basically similar to the 250cc Arrow Super Sports model. (Below)

Puch of Austria, one of the pioneer builders of motorcycles of the world. Shown here are several of their latest models. Puch also manufactures bikes for Sears Roebuck & Co., who market them under the trade name of Allstate. (Bottom)

49

NEW MOTOPLAS SCREEN

The latest Motoplas screen, the Weatherbetta, has a universal fitting for all lightweight motorcycles and a reversed curvatured top to break up air flow at eye level. (Below)

PEUGEOT BB104 FULLY AUTOMATIC MOPED

A highlight of the NSU/Layford stand at the Cycle and Motorcycle Exhibition at Earls Court, London, was this Peugeot BB104 two-seater moped. The BB104 is undoubtedly one of the most advanced mopeds in the world, for it has fully-automatic clutch and gear change—just like the most expensive motorcars. Starting is simply a matter of a push of the pedals. The BB104 will carry two in comfort at speeds of up to 40 m.p.h. and will return a fuel consumption of around 140 mpg. It has generous mudguarding and weather protection shield so that the driver keeps clean and dry. (Top right)

HONDA RANGE FOR 1965   C.95

The Honda C.95 150cc is the ideal all-purpose motorcycle. The C.95 has an electric starter similar to that on other Honda machines, a 4-speed gearbox, and produces 13.5 brake horsepower all from a twin cylinder 150cc overhead camshaft engine. The engine is whisper quiet and vibration free. The C.95 has all the important Honda extras at no extra cost, big brakes, rock-steady stability at all speeds on any type of road, handlebar mirrors and direction indicators. (Bottom)

Here, outside Buckingham Palace, is Mary of the American folk-singing trio Peter, Paul and Mary taking a look at the sights of London by motorcycle. Home in New York, Mary and her photographer-husband, Barry Fernstein, share a British Triumph 500cc machine in the hurly-burly of the city's traffic. As the easiest way of getting round London, she arranged for the Triumph firm at Coventry to loan her a 500cc Speed Twin. (Opposite page)

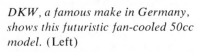

DKW, a famous make in Germany, shows this futuristic fan-cooled 50cc model. (Left)

Ducati of Italy offers this new folding Mini-Bike. At left is a four-cylinder Ducati experimental Apollo engine not yet in production. (Top left)

The new Italian Ducati "Diana" Super Sport. (Center left)

The new BSA 440cc Motorcross Victor has a long-stroke engine. (Below)

Jawa 125cc Roadster (Below center)

Italy produces some unique vehicles such as this Afe 175cc light truck. (Bottom)

Triumph T-120/R Bonneville has twin carbs, 40 cu. in. displacement. (Top left)

The Peugeot BB1C with 50cc engine is made in France and has automatic transmission. (Center)

More than 100,000 of these unit construction engines and gearboxes, here seen in the 200cc Tiger Cub, have been produced by the Triumph Engineering Co. at Meriden since the bike was introduced eleven years ago. Sports and trials versions of this very popular lightweight are also available. (Bottom)

Fashion Setter—Lambretta
Three of the very latest Lambretta scooters, comprising the new J-Range, are being introduced at the International Cycle & Motor Show at Earls Court. They are the J-50, the Cento 100 and the J125. Fashion models Diane Wilkinson and David Platt are wearing the latest Hardy Amies styles.

There is no easier way of touring places of interest in busy cities than on an economical scooter with automatic transmission. Modern Coventry, near the home of the 100cc Triumph Tina, is a case in point and all visitors to the city seem to make Coventry's cathedral their first priority. (Following page)

Hildebrand and Wolfmuller motor-cycle was manufactured in Munich, Germany, in 1894. It features a two-cylinder engine with connecting rods operating a gear-driven rear wheel. It has jump-spark ignition and the rear fender forms a tank for water cooling the engine.
Country: *Germany.* Maker: *Hilde-brand & Wolfmuller.* Date: *1894.*
Dimensions: *L. 6 ft. 6 in.*
W. 2 ft. 1-3/4 in. H. 3 ft. 6 in.
Wheelbase: 51 in. Dia. front wheel: 1 ft. 10-1/2 in. Dia. rear wheel: 1 ft. 6 in. Description: *Hildebrand & Wolfmuller motorcycle, black with gold striping. No front fender. Marked on sides of rear fender:* HILDEBRAND & WOLFMULLER, MUNCHEN. *Two-cylinder engine with connecting rods joined to solid rear wheel. Jump-spark ignition. The rear fender is a tank for water to cool engine.*

Shown here are a few of the many motorcycles on display in the famous Henry Ford Museum and Greenfield Village in Dearborn, Michigan. The photos are through the courtesy of the Museum.

- *This 1903 Aster has a one cylinder four-cycle engine, single tube tires and jump-spark ignition. A chain is utilized to turn the rear wheel to start the engine. The Aster was a French make but a few early Aster engines were imported to the United States and used in Orient motorcycles built in Waltham, Massachusetts, and the machine was marketed as an Orient-Aster. The first motorcycle sold in Los Angeles was purchased by Earl Lemoine and it was an Orient-Aster.*
Country: *United States.* Date: *1903.* Dimensions: *L. 6 ft. 5 in. H. 3 ft. 3-1/4 in. W. 1 ft. 11-1/2 in. Wheelbase: 49 in. Dia. wheels: 2 ft. 1 in.* Description: *Aster motorcycle,* dark blue with yellow striping, no fenders. 1 cylinder, 4-cycle engine No. E. 3724. Single tube tire. Belt driven on left. Jump-spark ignition. Chain on right side. Marked on engine between stars: ASTER/E 3274. (Top)

- *This 1904 Indian was manufactured by Hendee, Springfield, Massachusetts. The first Indians were powered by Thor engines built in Aurora, Illinois. This bike has a battery ignition and three dry-cell batteries and the coil all shown in the round containers mounted on the front frame tube. It was a four-cycle engine with automatic intake valve.*
Country: *United States (Springfield, Massachusetts).* Maker: *Hendee Mfg. Company.* Dimensions: *L. 6 ft. 3 in. H. 3 ft. 1 in. W. 2 ft. 1 in.* Wheelbase: *3 ft. 11 in. Dia. wheels: 1 ft., 10 in.* Description: *Indian Motorcycle, dark blue, marked in gold with red outline on each side of gasoline tank:* INDIAN/HENDEE MFG. CO./ SPRINGFIELD, MASS. *1 cylinder, 4-cycle, air-cooled engine marked:* HEDSTROM MOTOR./1081/HENDEE MFG. CO. SPRINGFIELD MASS. U.S.A. *Metal chain each side rear wheel to pedals. Leather oblong box between handlebars marked:* INDIAN. *Brown leather saddle seat marked:* PAT. FEB. 23, 1909, *insignia each side of seat shows Indian head within double circle marked:* INDIAN MOTORCYCLE THE HENDEE MANUFACTURING CO.

SPRINGFIELD MASS. *Remarks: In 1909 the gas tank of this motorcycle and the seat were changed from the original of 1904. (Bottom, opposite)*

• *This 4-1/2 h.p. Greyhound was built in Buffalo, New York. It was the successor to the Thomas Auto-Bi. Note the spring suspension seat-post which was unique for its time.* Country: *United States (Buffalo, N.Y.)* Maker: *Greyhound Motor Works.* Date: *1910.* Dimensions: *L. 7 ft. 1/2 in. H. 3 ft. 7 in. W. 2 ft. 3 in* Wheelbase: *56 in.* Dia. wheels: *2 ft.* Description: *Greyhound motorcycle, grey with black striping, marked each side of tank in black:* GREYHOUND/ BUFFALO/ N.Y. U.S.A. *1 cylinder, 4-1/2 h.p., 3-1/4 x 3-5/8*

in., engine placed vertically. Double Greyhound cushion forks; double grip, internal control; Breeze special carburetor; eclipse rear hub; ignition from battery. Metal chain on right rear wheel to pedal, leather strap on left rear wheel to pedal. Brake lever on left. No. 10159. (Top)

• *This 1910 Curtiss was manufactured in Hammondsport, New York, by the famous pioneer aviator and manufacturer, Glenn H. Curtiss. Mr. Curtiss was also the builder of the Marvel motorcycle which was similar. This unique engine had an odd overhead valve mechanism. A V-belt was used with an Eclipse clutch mounted in the front pulley. No doubt during restoration one "s" was dropped from*

the name on the tank, but the correct spelling is with two "s's." It has a Bosch magneto. Country: *United States (Hammondsport, N.Y.)* Maker: *Curtiss Motorcycle Manufacturing Co.* Date: *1910.* Dimensions: *L. 7 ft. 1 in. H. 3 ft. 6-1/2 in. W. 2 ft.* Wheelbase: *2 ft. Dia. front wheel: 1 ft. 11-3/4 in. Dia. rear wheel: 2 ft.* Description: *Curtiss Motorcycle, olive green with gold striping, marked each side of tank in gold with red outline:* CURTISS MOTORCYCLE MFG. CO./ HAMMONDSPORT N.Y. U.S.A. *One cylinder, air-cooled engine marked:* CURTISS MOTOR/ MODEL G. NO. *6030. Firestone tires 28 x 2-1/2. Black leather saddle seat. Leather-*

strap on left side rear wheel to pedal, metal chain on right side to pedal. (Bottom, previous page)

- *Few people know that Charles A. Lindbergh, the pioneer aviator and first New York to Paris flyer, was an enthusiastic motorcycle rider. Colonel Lindbergh gave his motorcycle to the museum where it is now displayed. It is a Series 20 Excelsior 61 Cubic Engine Twin that was manufactured in the fall of 1919. The bike is a light blue and has a Berling magneto and a Schebler carburetor. The kick-starter pedal is shown on the left and the three-speed gearshift lever is mounted alongside the gasoline tank. On the handlebars is a Prest-O-Lite tank which furnished acetylene gas* for the headlight. Lindbergh used this motorcycle when he was an airmail pilot flying out of St. Louis, Missouri, and during his barnstorming days of the early twenties, and also after his famous flight.

Country: *United States (Chicago, Ill.)* Maker: *Excelsior Motor Manufacturing & Supply Co.* Date: *1919. Model 20. Purchased by Lindbergh in 1919.* Dimensions: *H. approx. 3 ft. 6-1/2 in. L. approx. 7 ft. 4-1/2 in.* Wheelbase: *approx. 58-1/2 in.* Dia. wheels: *20 in.* Description: *Motorcycle finished in original colors: blue, gray wheels, and yellow striping. Original decals applied. Brown saddle marked:* MESINGER/1 *in a circle/*CUSHION SUSPENSION.

Brass lamp in front; Prestoline tank. Tool box. Stand. Two-cylinder engine: 4-speed transmission; final chain drive. Cycle is completely authentic except for distributor control installed by Lindbergh. Remarks: *Restored by Ted Hodgdon, Nutley, N.J., on contract, January, 1962. Hodgdon is president of the Antique Motorcycle Club. Cycle owned by Charles A. Lindbergh.* Source: *Gift of Charles A. Lindbergh.* (Top)

- *1929 Cleveland. This was one of the few four-cylinder motorcycles manufactured in the United States. Only a few ever reached the market. The four-cylinder in-line engine was air cooled. This company were quite*

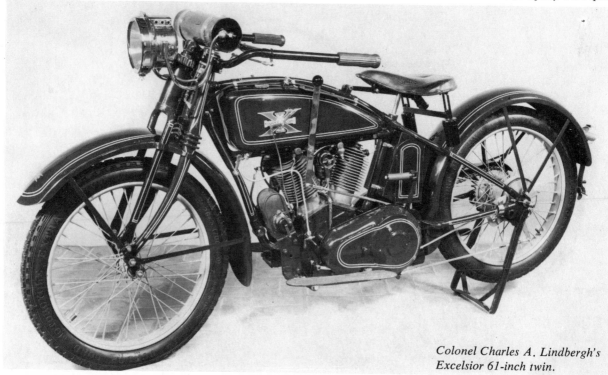

Colonel Charles A. Lindbergh's Excelsior 61-inch twin.

large manufacturers of single cylinder two-cycle motorcycles and they certainly stubbed their toe when they tried to enter the big machine market with a four-cylinder job.

Country: *United States (Cleveland, Ohio.)* Maker: *The Cleveland Motorcycle Manufacturing Co.* Date: *1929.* Dimensions: *L. 7 ft. 5-1/4 in. H. 3 ft. 7 in. W. 3 ft.* Wheelbase: *4 ft. 10 in. Dia. wheels: 1 ft. 8-3/4 in.* Description: *Cleveland motorcycle, dark blue with gold striping marked each side of tank:* CLEVELAND/ (*in a circle with wings each side*) 4. *Light in front. Four cylinders, air cooled, motor number J. S. 1110 A. Plate on engine marked:* CLEVELAND (*in a circle with wings each side*) 4/WE

RECOMMEND/FOR/ENGINE GARGOYLE MOBIL "BB" SUMMER/GARGOYLE MOBILOIL "A" WINTER/FOR TRANSMISSION GARGOYLE MOBILOIL "BB"/THE CLEVELAND MOTORCYCLE MFG. CO./CLEVELAND, U.S.A. *Foot pedals marked:* CLEVELAND. *1930 Michigan license on rear. 27 x 4.00 pneumatic tires. Magneto. Gift of Raymond C. Dahlinger.* (Bottom, previous page)

• *This 1913 Thor was manufactured by the Aurora Automatic Machinery Company in Aurora, Illinois, who manufactured motorcycle engines that were used by many U.S. manufacturers in their early days, including the first Indians. This two-cylinder engine has 7 horsepower*

and 61 cubic inches displacement. A two-speed transmission is mounted in the rear wheel. The machine, as yet, is unrestored.

Country: *United States (Aurora, Illinois).* Maker: AURORA AUTOMATIC MACHINERY CO. Date: *1913.* Dimensions: *L. 7 ft. 5 in. W. 1 ft. 11 in. H. 3 ft. 6 in.* Wheelbase: *57 in.* Description: *Thor motorcycle, white, marked in blue and silver on left side of tank:* THOR AURORA AUTO MCHG. CO. AURORA ILL. *Marked same in blue and gold on right side. Lamp in front. Two cylinders, 7 h.p., 2 speeds. Brown leather saddle seat, marked with wings:* TROXEL MFG./ ELYRIA O. U.S.A. *Source: Gift of F. W. Thomas.* (Top)

• Latest gift to the Ford Museum was by the Honda Motor Co., Ltd., of Japan and American Honda Motor Company, Inc., of Gardena, California. It is the famed Honda R.C. 161 Grand Prix racing bike. It has a four-cylinder double overhead cam engine with four valves per cylinder. It develops 47 h.p. at 14,500 r.p.m.'s. It has a six-speed constant mesh fast shift transmission. These machines were victorious in nearly every race in which they entered, and in 1961 captured first, second, third, fourth and fifth places in the 250cc World Points with a perfect 48 point score. Source: Gift of Honda Motor Co., Ltd., Japan, and American Honda Motor Co. Gardena, California.

Country: Japan. Condition: Like new. Artist or Maker: Honda Motor Co., Ltd., Japan. Date and Period: 1961. Dimensions: Length: 75 in. Road Clearance: 6¼ in. Wheelbase: 51 in. Width: 21 in. Height: 42 in. Weight: 228 lbs. wet Description: Frame: Arc-welded tubular steel with backbone main tube and sub-tubes. Front Suspension: Telescopic type, hydraulically dampened spring. Brakes: Internal-expanding full width—light alloy hubs with 7.1 in. dia. drums. Engine: 4 cylinders, double overhead cam, 4 valves per cylinder, 47 h.p. @ 14,500 rpm, 18,000 rpm,

6-speed constant mesh transmission, 3.33 Total Primary Reduction. (Bottom, previous page)

Until about 1950, rigid-rear suspension was universal on most production motorcycles. In this early Triumph, for instance, axle was bolted directly into rear frame for rigid and then conventional system. (Below left)

New Honda CL-77 Scrambler has well braced rear suspension, with near vertical location of enclosed spring unit. (Below right)

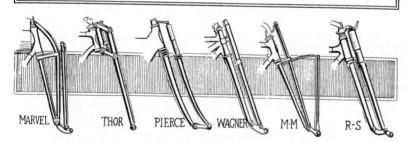

A HALF DOZEN TYPES OF 1911 FORKS

MARVEL   THOR   PIERCE   WAGNER   M·M   R-S

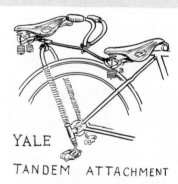

YALE

TANDEM ATTACHMENT

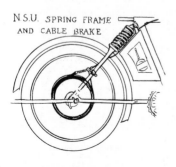

N.S.U. SPRING FRAME AND CABLE BRAKE

SPRING SEAT POST

"R-S"

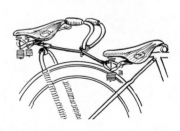

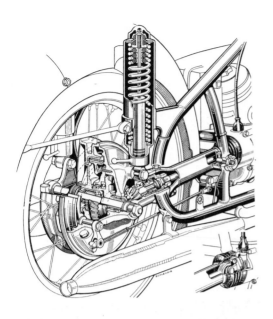

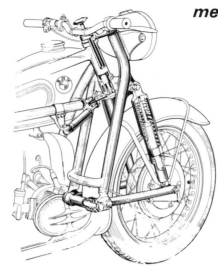

Throughout the years there have been many different designs of rear and front-wheel suspension and we are illustrating some of the most popular ones, both old and new.

BSA uses modern design of enclosed rear springing with near vertical location of the unit.

Yamaha uses open springs on their modern rear swing-arm suspension— note angle of spring location.

The cradle spring-frame rear suspension system was used in Indian models from 1913 to the early twenties.

Today's production motorcycle offers well-controlled ride through vast improvements in suspension. Changes have made sport safer and more comfortable for beginners and experts alike. Yet a few "custom" bikes (like this ?) are stripped down. High handlebars do not offer good control of bike. (Left)

This production Honda features leading link front suspension in which springs occupy pressed steel legs and are tied at midpoint of link itself. (Below left)

Rear suspension system on Spanish Montesa. (Below right.)

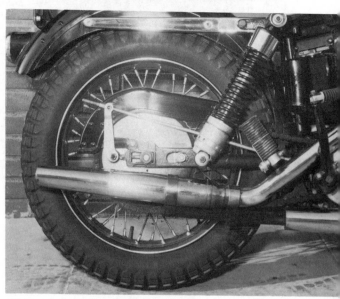

This variation on the Harley-Davidson Sportster swinging-arm rear suspension system puts spring-shock connection part way along arm itself; axle is further back and not directly connected to springshock. (Above)

A drawing by Moto-Revue of Paris of a unique British Norton racing bike. (Right)

A well-defined leading link system is the Earles fork on this BMW. Long links to axle come forward from fork legs well to the rear. Note massive spring-shock legs. (Below left)

Swinging arm rear suspension with combined spring and shock absorber started a new trend in early 1950's. This system is now almost universal for production machines. Note well-designed luggage carrier. (Below center)

Yamaha rear suspension system. (Below right)

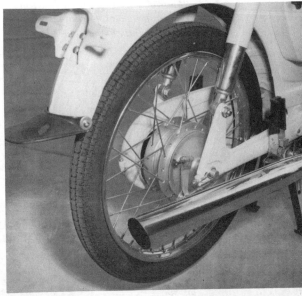

Hydraulically damped (telescopic) forks provide ideal combination of ruggedness, safety and rider comfort. Lower fork section of this Triumph slides up and over long tubes attached to steering head. Some designs include coil springs inside tubes, others prefer large springs outside. These suspensions can be custom tailored to rider's preference and type of usage by changing spring weights. (Right)

Cutaway of Ariel Pixie front suspension. (Far right)

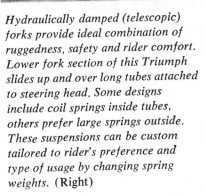

This heavily chromed Triumph engine has unusually short exhaust stacks, and a small saddle with no upholstering. While these bikes are seldom practical, they do attract much attention when placed on exhibition.

Shown here are some illustrations of some well-known motorcycle engines.

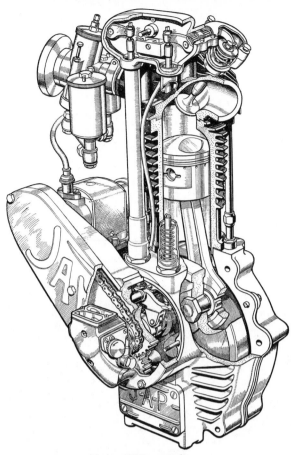

The J.A.P. Speedway 550cc engine.
For many years, the J.A.P. has
dominated most speedway or short
track events.

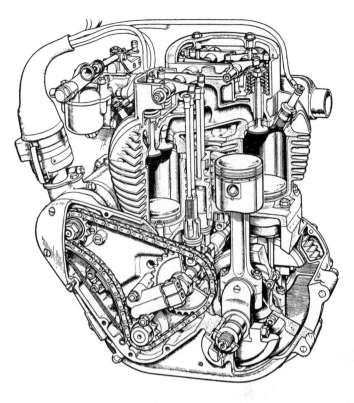

For years, the Ariel "Square Four"
was popular, due to the quiet and
smoothness of operation. These bikes
are now collector's items, as they
are no longer manufactured.

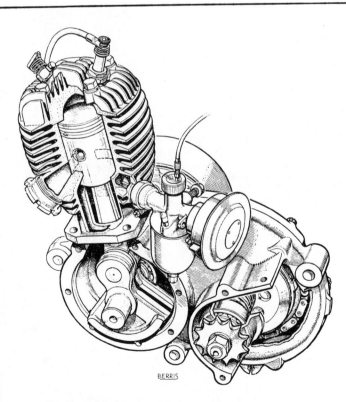

The Villiers Company of England
has produced quality 2-cycle engines
for over 50 years. Shown here is a
98cc light-weight engine suitable
for Mopeds.

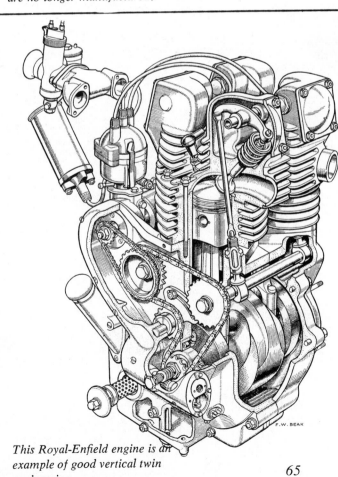

This Royal-Enfield engine is an
example of good vertical twin
engineering.

65

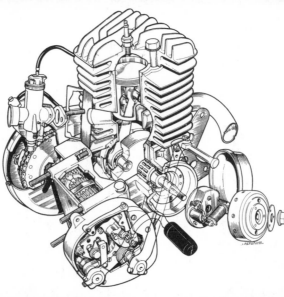

This BSA twin engine of unit construction has twin carburetors and 650cc capacity. It is used in Lightning and Hornet models. This is an example of fine British engineering of a vertical twin engine, in which the entire transmission and clutch are incorporated in a single unit power plant. (Far left)

The new Greeves 250cc "Challenger" is an outstanding performing 2-cycle engine. (Left)

This Triumph racing engine with dual carburetors was prepared by Barney Macias for use on Bonneville, Utah, Salt Flats competition. (Below)

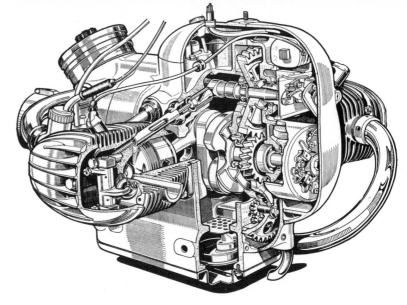

BMWs are famous for their opposed
twin engines, and they are an
example of fine engineering.
Model is the R-60, with 600cc
displacement which develops 30 hp.

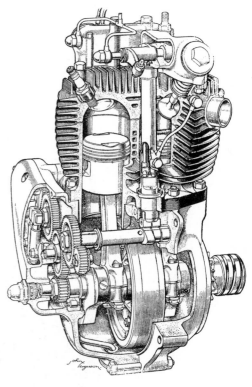

The Triumph Thunderbird 650cc
vertical twin engine is an example of
unique design, and is popular in
the United States. (Above)

An example of fine Japanese
engineering is this two-stroke
Yamaha single engine. (Top left)

Note unique exhaust pipe of this
potent 250cc Spanish Montesa
2-cycle engine. (Left)

In early years of motorcycling there was very little available in the way of special equipment. Today, however, the cyclist has a wide selection of special equipment such as accessories and parts, riding apparel, helmets, gloves and other equipment. The rider will do well to select riding apparel that will offer the best in comfort and utility. It is impossible to illustrate all of the fine special equipment available, however, we are illustrating some of the equipment that is most popular.

Hitch-Hiker for Lightweights. Model H. H. Accurate Accessories. Bolts on to trailer hitch to carry cycle outside car. Chain and lock clamp rear wheel to rack, bike centerstand supports weight at hitch.

Bungee cords have plastic covered hooks for fast, sure tie-downs to saddle or pack-rack. Various colors, 18-inch and 24-inch lengths available. Webco.

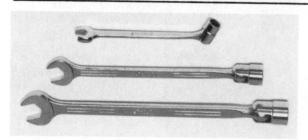

Metric Combination Wrenches— Webco. Set of three wrenches with open end and swivel socket for greatest convenience and versatility. Sizes are 10mm, 14mm, 17mm.

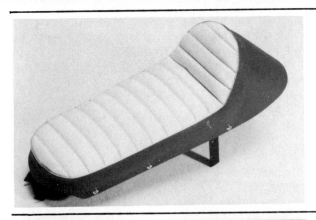

Grand Prix Saddle—Webco. Fiber-glass molded base with extremely lightweight foam rubber cushion, durable Naugahyde cover. Brackets for universal mounting included.

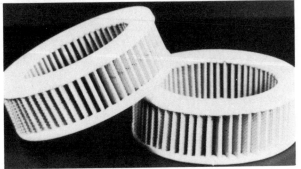

Washable Air Cleaner Element—Webco. May be washed off in solvent and re-used. Designed specifically for off-highway use where dust is a constant problem. Light film of oil may be added for even greater efficiency. Polyfoam edging assures perfect seal. Fits all 6¼-inch diameter cleaners.

Jet Plate—Webco. Cast and machined aluminum alloy plate holds twenty main jets for easy identification. Ideal for tuners, travelers. Also available for regular Amal-carbs, Dell'Orto and Honda.

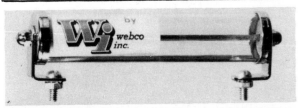

Registration Certificate Holder—Webco. Watertight, chrome-plated holder enables mounting of registration on license plate, rear fender, etc. Complete with brackets, attaching screws, nuts. From Webco, or at most dealers.

Folding Foot Pegs—Bates. Available in competition style as shown, for welding to frame or cut-down stock peg. Also good for trail bikes. Folds up to prevent leg injury. Also available in bolt-on style or with clamps to mount on frame for passenger pegs. Various models, including economy style.

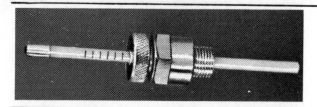

Piston Position Indicator—Webco. For setting spark lead, checking cam timing. Screws into 14mm spark plug hole on hemi-head design engines. Sliding nylon rod graduated in ⅛-inch increments. May be used with dial indicator.

Cast Aluminum Taillight Fairing— Bates. Highly polished, modern sculptured design with hood over lens. Taillight, 6V or 12V, red plastic lens. Chromed license plate holder.

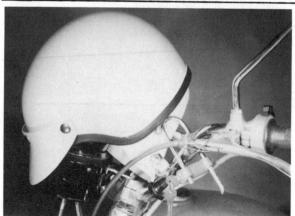

Helmet Lock—Bates. Protects against helmet theft. Lock to helmet "D" ring and handlebar, frame, etc.

Bates Saddle. Cross Country—Long, low, and heavily cushioned. Designed for desert racing as shown here on 1964 Triumph racing mount. Also popular with comfort-seeking road riders.

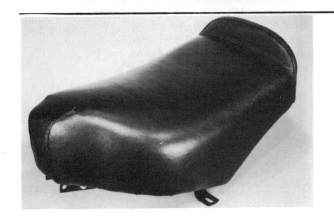

Bates Saddle. TT—Short, with close-in rear support, thick cushioning needed for control and comfort in jumps, turns.

Accurate Accessories for Trail Models. Yamaha shown is equipped with A-A Pack Rack Sr. Rack fits most existing bolt holes. Fits Yamaha YG-1, YG-1T, MJ-2 Trail, YDS2, YDT-1, Suzuki 80, Gilera, and 1964 Triumph Cub. Pack Rack Jr. is slightly smaller. Buddy seat with strap in black only. High bars with cross-brace are Model HB-1. Also available at same angle, but lower, in Model LB-1. Same bars less cross-brace are Models HB-2 and LB-2. Rifle Carrier (less scabbard) mounts on existing fittings. Motor Shield Sr. for Yahama YG-1 and YG1-T protects engine from rocks, stumps and other off-road hazards. Chrome plated for beauty as well as function. Motor Shield Jr. does not have upper loop to frame. Most Accurate Accessories fit popular Honda models as well.

Sprocket Carrier Ring—Webco. For Honda 50, 55, 90cc models. Alloy carrier mounts on standard hub assembly to carry overlay sprocket when not in use, permitting change without removal of rear wheel. System is similar to that on latest Honda trail model.

Metal Float Needle—Webco. Replaces nylon needle supplied in Amal Monobloc. Eliminates flooding, excessive top rpm leanness.

Air Cleaner Lock Nut—Webco. Alloy ring is precision machined with driving slots for tight mounting of air cleaner. Safety screw prevents loosening from vibration. No. 1072 fits 15/16 to 11/16-inch, No. 1073 fits 13/32 to 13/16-inch models.

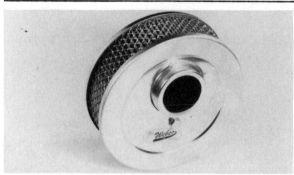

Air Cleaner—Webco. Slips over threaded carburetor inlet, uses air-horn or lock nut to secure cleaner to carb. Diameter is 6-1/4 inches, 2 inches thick. Includes No. 1116 paper pack element. A fits 21/32 to 7/8 inch. B fits 15/16 to 11/16 inch, C fits 13/32 to 13/16 inch.

Neoprene Mixing Chamber Cover Cap—Webco. Fits snugly around carburetor body and throttle cable to prevent all foreign matter from entering through slide cover cap or cable inlet. Acts as lock to keep cap from loosening due to vibration. Resistant to heat, gasoline and oil. No. 1449 fits 1-1/16 in. carb, No. 1450 fits 1-3/16 in. model.

Float Bowl Extension—Webco. Increases bowl capacity by 50 per cent. Ideal for sustained rpm with large displacement engines.

Windshields—Bates. Heavy, shatter-proof plastic with greatest resistance to impact. Optically clear and curved for greater strength. Edges reinforced with patented plastic bead. Trim is stainless and hardware is highly polished chrome. Sizes vary, with widths running 12, 15, 18, and 22 inches. Blue or red plastic lower portion if requested, no extra charge. Replacement parts available.

Shown here are three Harley-Davidson factories. At top and center are the USA factories at Milwaukee and Butler; and below is a photo of the Aermacchi Harley-Davidson plant in Varese, Italy, where Harley-Davidson Sprint and M-50 models are produced. Harley-Davidson owns 49% interest in this Italian factory. Aermacchi also manufactures airplanes and precision aircraft parts.

Harley-Davidson golf carts and trucks—Harley-Davidson also manufactures a line of three-wheel vehicles that are used by golfers, motels, business firms, factories and for many other commercial uses. (Right top and bottom)

there's always something new

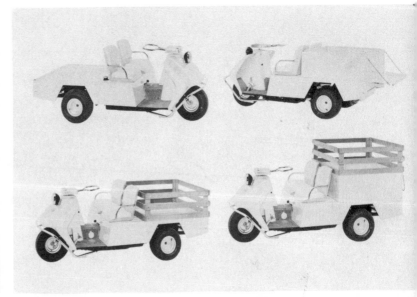

The 4-cylinder Benelli streamlined racer is one of Italy's new fast combination bikes. (Bottom)

The Harley-Davidson "Topper" scooter has a 2-cycle engine with a pull-up hand starter and automatic transmission. (Left)

The Marusho Opposed Twin from Japan. This bike from Japan has 500cc engine. It is almost a duplicate of the German BMW engine, but with smaller engine capacity. (Center)

These two Mobylettes from France are now entering the U.S. market. Mobylette is the largest manufacturer of motorcycles in France. (Right and upper left on opposite page)

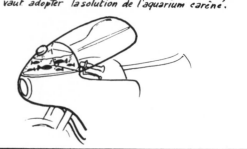

Vous partez en vacances à moto. Votre chat, votre chien vous pouvez les emmener, ou les mettre à la fourrière. Mais, avez-vous pensé à vos poissons rouges? Personne n'en veut, c'est immangeable; évidemment vous pouvez lesdonner au chat, lui s'arrangera toujours pour les transporter. Mieux vaut adopter la solution de l'aquarium caréné.

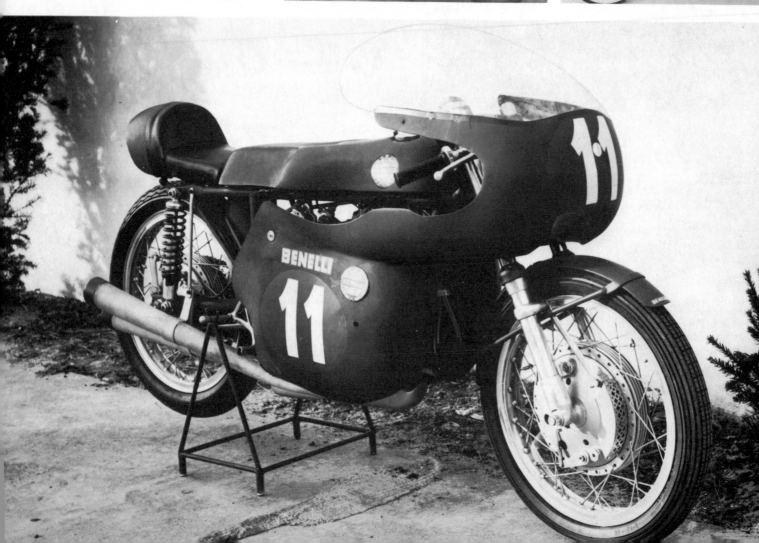

Humor from France. Frenchmen always have a sense of humor as evidenced by these cartoons from Moto-Revue. On the left is a group of goldfish in the front part of the windscreen. The lady passenger on the right is enjoying a built-in television set in the helmet of the rider. Must be a sad picture as evidenced by the look on her face.

This Bultaco 175cc "Sherpa Scrambler" is making new friends for this popular Spanish make. (Top right)

Jawa also markets the famous ESO 500cc Dirttrack Racer—one of the fastest in the world. (Bottom left)

Unorthodox JAWA Moto-cross "works" Model. (Bottom right)

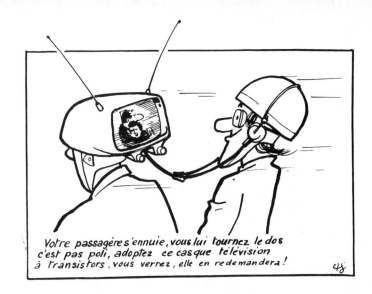

Votre passagère s'ennuie, vous lui tournez le dos c'est pas poli, adoptez ce casque télévision à transistors, vous verrez, elle en redemandera!

Fairings are now popular and available for all makes of motorcycles—shown here is a BMW. (Above)

UNIQUE CUSTOM CONVERSION—*The Strucher-Steinebech Crosley-Yamaha. This 900cc four-cylinder water-cooled Crosley car engine is fitted to a Yamaha chassis.* (Left)

Competition minded Jawa of Czechoslovakia has won many competition events with this 350cc overhead camshaft road racer. (Opposite page left)

The popularity of Spanish makes has increased rapidly in the past few months. Shown here is the Bultaco 250cc Metisse lightweight model. The crates on the truck contain Spanish Montesa machines for the importer. (Top and center left)

Greeves of England have had exceptional success in the United States and other countries with their famous competition bikes such as this 250cc Challenger Scrambler. (Bottom left)

Benelli, built by the largest Italian factory, is now being imported and sold in the United States. (Top right)

Yamaha has an injection system called "Autolube" which injects the correct quantity of oil into the induction system necessary for their 2-cycle engine. (Center right)

Jawa of Czechoslovakia has a wide range of models and is sold in over 100 countries throughout the world. Jawa and CZ (built by Jawa) riders have won many championships throughout the world and are many times winners of famous Six Day Trials. (Bottom right)

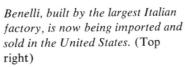

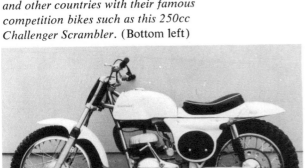

Yamaha of Japan recently introduced
this new "Trailmaster 80." (Right)

Honda's new CB-160 Model now
available in the U.S. (Top left)

Garelli is a quality product built in
Italy, now being imported to the
U.S. (Bottom left)

Tempo is a new bike from Denmark.
Shown here is the nicely finished and
designed Tempo equipped with a
German Sachs engine. (Center right)

The new Italian Ducati fan-cooled
trail bike. (Bottom right)

While it has nothing to do with motorcycles, Honda also manufactures this special generator. (Left)

Harley-Davidson Racers. The racer shown below left at bottom is the 45-cubic-inch V-Twin racer and the 250cc Sprint built in Italy for Harley-Davidson.

Cushman of Lincoln, Nebraska, offers many different types of three-wheel commercial vehicles. (Below right)

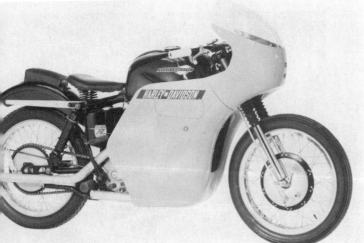

This Mustang trail bike is one of the few American makes available to the United States buyer. (Left)

The world's factories are barely meeting motorcycle demand. This is Yahama, in Japan. (Center left)

Even little Holland is in the act and has recently imported several different models of the Sparta. (Center right)

This is a drawing of the new Yamaha International Corporation's plant at Montebello, California. The cost exceeded one million dollars, and the plant occupies 53,000 feet of floor space. (Bottom)

A piano may look out of place in this book, but Yamaha claims to be the largest builders of pianos in the world. They are sold in the United States. Yamaha also builds outboard motors—not sold in the U.S. market.

Motorcycle competition is well controlled in the United States. Throughout the years there have been three large organizations in the States to control and sanction motorcycle competition. Soon after the turn of the century the first was the Federation of American Motorcyclists and for years the offices were in New England.

In the first half of the 1920's, motorcycle manufacturers and allied trades members felt that they should have more direct control of competition events so the Motorcycle and Allied Trades Association was formed. The M.A.T.A., under Chairman A. B. Coffman, was the governing body and issued sanctions during the early 1920's. The directors of this association felt that there should also be a rider organization so the competition division was turned over to the newly formed American Motorcycle Association; thus the F.A.M., M.A.T.A., and the AMA have been the continuing bodies that govern motorcycle activities in the United States.

From time to time other organizations have attempted to sanction motorcycle competition, but most of them have been unsuccessful. About 1916 there was a Western Federation of Motorcyclists in Los Angeles which seceded from the parent F.A.M. In the 1950's, the United States Motorcycle Club was formed. They worked in cooperation with the FIM, which is the international body governing motorcycle competition throughout the world. The FIM and the AMA, however, have never been affiliated, and FIM competition riders in the United States do not ride in AMA events but have competed in races

sanctioned by the U.S.M.C. and the American Association of Motorcycle Road Racers. The AAMRR has operated under FIM rules in many road racing events held mostly in the Eastern states and Florida.

The AMA is the largest and the dominating association in the United States. The current President is William E. Kennedy and the Executive Secretary is Lin Kuchler. The home office is in Columbus, Ohio. In recent years, the AMA has developed a very effective public relations department that does much to create good will for motorcyclists.—F.C.

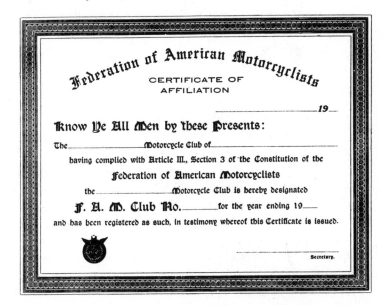

In 1908 the membership certificate of the first U.S. Motorcycle Association looked like this. It was the Federation of American Motorcyclists.

Lin Kuchler, A.M.A. Executive Secretary.

by LIN KUCHLER
A.M.A. Executive Secretary

The year was 1903. The place was Brooklyn, New York, where 92 motorcycle enthusiasts had gathered to attend a meeting of the New York Motorcycle Club and the Alpha Motorcycle Club. The meeting was optimistically billed as a "convention," despite the slim attendance.

Of the members present, 44 contributed $2 each for membership fees, thus becoming founders of the Federation of American Motorcyclists.

This humble beginning actually was the forerunner of today's American Motorcycle Association now headquartered in Columbus, Ohio, which directs the activities of over 75,000 motorcyclists.

Actually, the AMA was organized in its approximate present form in 1924, thus making 1965 the 41st year of its existence. But it was the early impetus of the Federation of American Motorcyclists which banded together the motorcycle enthusiasts into an organized group.

Much has transpired since this small pioneer group of motorcycle fans convened. The AMA today sanctions more than 3,800 separate motorcycle events annually, both for prize money and for cups and medals in the Sportsman category. About 10 per cent of the total is in the well-publicized "Formula C" racing program. The total also includes some 3,500 Sportsman events which draw on the average of 50 riders per event.

Equally important is the supervision by the AMA of over 1,350 chartered motorcycle clubs ranging in size from a dozen members to over 100 enthusiasts, which form the backbone of the Association's program.

Born in a modest fashion, the AMA today is housed in a modern Columbus, Ohio office building where a staff of four men and 12 women coordinate the many activities of the Association. Directing the staff is Secretary Lin Kuchler, genial and efficient "exec," whose background in motorcycle sports and in business qualifies him well for this demanding job. Other male members of the staff include a Competition Director, who issues thousands of sanctions annually, and who keeps a finger on scheduling of all races. A Club Director makes contact with the 1,350 clubs representing AMA membership throughout the nation. An accountant, who works closely with the executive secretary, watches over the billing procedures and all other financial matters including the membership program. Since the installation of the very latest Addressograph equipment in 1960, the continuous flow of memberships is now processed on a daily basis, and all members receive convenient renewal envelope reminders approximately 30 days before their membership expires.

Proof of the stability of the AMA is evidenced in the fact that each year over 150 members become 25-year "life" members. This group, now numbering 1,900, includes some of the greatest names in motorcycle history, many of them famous competition riders.

Since its inception as the AMA in 1924, the Association has had three executive secretaries

Typical A.M.A. District Referee is Dick Gardner, Kansas State Referee. Striped shirt is usually worn. (Left)

and six presidents. Kuchler was preceded by E. C. Smith in the secretary's post. Smith's predecessor was A. B. Coffman.

Current President William E. Kennedy, Manager of Distribution, Roller Chain Division, Rex Chainbelt, Inc., Springfield, Massachusetts, was elected February 17, 1965 as the sixth president of the American Motorcycle Association. Preceding him in office have been Carl T. Swenson (February 10, 1954-February 17, 1965), president of Milsco Mfg. Co. of Milwaukee, Wisconsin; George D. Gilbert (January 18, 1951-February 10, 1954) at that time president of the Baldwin-Duckworth Co. of Springfield, Massachusetts; Arthur Davidson (January 19, 1944-December 30, 1950) one of the founders of the Harley-Davidson Motor Co., Milwaukee, Wisconsin; James A. Wright (February 4, 1928-January 19, 1944) at that time sales and advertising manager of the Indian Motorcycle Co., Springfield, Massachusetts. First president of the American Motorcycle Association was George T. Briggs (1924-February 4, 1928) of the Wheeler-Schebler Carburetor Co.

The complete club file in Columbus reveals that the AMA members cover the entire gamut of ages and professions—ranging from youngsters learning to ride their first machine, to "oldsters" who have ridden for as long as 50 years. And noticeably sprinkled thruout the membership roster are many professional people—doctors, lawyers, schoolteachers—all of whom have found motorcycling a wholesome, thrilling diversion.

A valuable adjunct to the AMA is its 30-member Competition Committee, a group of enthusiasts all active in some phase or other of motorcycling, appointed annually by the Executive Secretary with approval of the AMA's Trustees. These men, who represent a collective total of well over 500 years of motorcycle experience, consider, formulate, adopt and amend rules, based on the suggestions of members of the AMA, including recommendations of many competition riders. Members of the Committee, all of whom serve gratis, have been selected on the basis of thorough knowledge of the sport as a result of their backgrounds as dealers, representatives of various foreign and domestic manufacturers, or,

A.M.A. COMPETITION COMMITTEE MEMBERS— This photo was taken at the annual meeting of the A.M.A. Competition Committee, held at the offices of The Triumph Corporation, Towson, Baltimore, Md. Officers change from year to year, but the present officers shown in the photo are (from L. to R.): Back Row—

Billy Temple, Dick O'Brien, Walt Brown, Leonard Andres, Pete Colman and Trevor Deeley; Middle Row— Jules Horky, Jim Davis, Bruce Walters, Rod Coates, Earl Widman, Oscar Lenz, Rabun Chambless, and Horace Fritz; Front Row—John Esler, James Tagaris, Ewin Warmack, L. A. Kuchler, John Aarvold, and

most important, as former competition riders. The Technical Committee, a highly qualified seven-man group, is entrusted with the mechanical, engineering and technical aspects of the AMA competition. This Committee is always represented at each major sanctioned motorcycle event.

Since its inception, the AMA has sanctioned a staggering total of more than 90,000 individual events, which would certainly indicate its experience in directing the activities of American motorcyclists.

In recent years, the AMA has developed a formal public relations program which is "bearing fruit" in increased national recognition of the sport in all its aspects by major television and radio networks, national sporting magazines, and the daily press of the nation. Such key "Nationals" as Daytona Beach, Florida; Springfield, Illinois; and Laconia, New Hampshire attract coverage from all the news capitals of the nation.

While the AMA has never *promoted* an event in its history, it sanctions these events in conjunction with such reputable and respected promoters as J. C. Agajanian, Eddie Witzenberg, Bill France of Daytona Beach fame and many others. These men have worked closely with the AMA for many years, and their efforts, plus the solid reputation of the sanctioning body has led to many successful promotions.

Another indication of the stability of the AMA is seen in the fact that some of its races have been on the AMA calendar for as long as 45 years, as is the case of the annual Laconia, New Hamp-

shire New England Tour and Rally, which is a promotion of a group of New England motorcycle dealers. Other veteran AMA dates include Daytona Beach, Florida, and Springfield, Illinois, which have hosted "Nationals" for some 30 years; Peoria, Illinois' "Tourist Trophy" National, which started in that city in 1947; and the Columbus, Ohio Charity Newsies which has been an AMA sanctioned race for some 15 years.

As in any sport, great names among the participants have helped make AMA history. Today's top figures include such riders as Roger Reiman, Grand National Champion; Dick Mann, Bart Markel, Ronnie Rall, Ralph White, George Roeder, Gary Nixon, Jody Nicholas, and many others. Their predecessors in motorcycling's mythical "hall of fame" include such names as Joe Petralli, who is one of the AMA's distinguished life members; Jim Davis of Columbus, still one of the most active AMA members in the country; Babe Tancrede, Dud Perkins, Oscar Lenz, Floyd Clymer, Hap Alzina, Windy Lindstrom, and many other luminaries from out of the past. And more recently; Brad Andres, Joe Leonard, Dick Klamfoth and Carroll Resweber.

Because one of the AMA's prime concerns is improving the status of its competition riders, the Association points with pride to its record of having increased purses considerably at Nationals over the years. This year's schedule of Nationals will offer total purses of some $120,000.00, the largest total in the history of the AMA's racing program.

While racing is admittedly the most noticeable

A meeting of A.M.A. officials in the fifties. Standing at left is President Carl Swensen, with William Davidson at the right. Seated left to right: Larry Paul, the president of the Indian Company; T. A. Hodgdon, president of BSA Incorporated; and Denis McCormack, president of The Triumph Corporation.

part of the AMA program, the Association actually devotes much of its time and effort to educational and informative liaison with clubs and dealers. Clubs are circularized frequently with material that will help them be more effective in their own areas. Dealers are given promotion and educational help, such as in the case of the very successful "Best Wheel Forward" program which acknowledged the vital importance of the dealer organization, and the recent AMA "Two-Wheeled Wisdom" safety film and safety brochures designed to promote motorcycle highway safety.

A complete motorcycle insurance program, known as "American Motorcycle Association Insurance Program," underwritten by the Midwest Mutual and Preferred Risk Mutual Insurance Companies, is made available to AMA members.

The Columbus headquarters office gets a steady stream of mail from members who need information on various phases of motorcycling. Sanctions for all forms of AMA events are issued from the AMA office. A large part of the Association's efforts to "reward" competition in the Sportsman class comes in the huge volume of AMA donated trophies and tour awards which riders receive for their participation.

The American Motorcycle Association, since its inception, has regarded safety as a prime consideration in all activities of its members. Races are conducted under the most stringent safety rules. Members of the Technical Committee must approve the equipment of each racing entrant before he may compete. The Competition Com-

mittee works closely with manufacturers to assure that helmets and other racing items are of the highest standards. And, perhaps most important, the AMA also has a strong club safety program, awarding safety banners annually to all clubs that can prove that they have not had any chargeable accidents during the year.

The editorial voice of the Association, *American Motorcycling Magazine,* is also housed in the Columbus headquarters. Besides the regular coverage of numerous competitive events, the magazine develops feature material on all phases of the sport, and makes frequent reprint mailings to clubs and dealers on subjects that are of unusual interest to all riders.

*Director of A.M.A. Competition—
Jules Horky.*

Typical couple are typical of "new image" cycle riders on their BSA.

The objectives of the AMA are many-fold. The Association stresses safety and good riding habits both among its competitors and its "enthusiast" members. It strives constantly to make the field of racing more attractive for competition riders and for spectators. It is strengthening its program each year by encouraging the motorcyclist to take part in civic and charitable activities and to play a bigger role in his own community affairs. The recognition the AMA and its members are now receiving indicates that motorcycling is gaining the increased stature it deserves.

The campaign theme "Put Your Best Wheel Forward," which the AMA features in all its promotional endeavors, best typifies the aims of the nation's oldest, largest, and most progressive motorcycle association.

TWO-WHEELED WISDOM:
Safety Hints

Your role as a motorcyclist includes adherence to safety rules, as well as dressing neatly and conducting yourself on the highway as a responsible member of the fraternity that promotes the "greatest sport on wheels." The American Motorcycle Association reminds you always to keep your "Best Wheel Forward."

Two-wheeled vehicles can add to the fun and wholesome entertainment of the open road. But the importance of safety cannot be stressed too greatly in the operation of any vehicles.

The American Motorcycle Association, which long has advocated "two-wheeled wisdom" in all cycling activities, would like to issue the following reminders to all cyclists, to make their two-wheeled activities more pleasurable, safer and better accepted by the public.

Starting

—Check all controls for proper operation. Then start your engine and allow it to properly warm up before proceeding in traffic. The miss of a cold engine could leave you in serious trouble.

Braking

—Braking a motorcycle takes a great deal of skill and common sense. Since the front brake of the two wheeler is the most powerful, apply the rear brake first, then ease down gently on the front one. Brake gently on slippery surfaces. Don't freeze at the controls. And remember always to use your brakes before rounding a turn, not while you are in it. And, of course, always make sure that your brakes are in proper adjustment. Remember also that with clutch engaged, your engine also acts as a brake when the throttle is closed.

To the beginning rider: to increase speed you turn the throttle IN (on) and to decrease speed you turn the throttle OUT (off). So a simple safety rhyme to remember is: *"When in doubt turn out."*

Stop Signs

—As you approach a stop sign, reduce your speed and let your engine deceleration act as a brake.

Gradually apply your rear wheel brake, follow up with your front wheel brake and shift down to a lower gear as you reduce to a safe down shifting speed. Do not set your front wheel brake before the rear wheel brake is fully set. Remember: "thinking distance and braking distance."

Coming to a full stop and looking both ways is a simple rule to follow at stop signs. There's nothing important enough to make you "run" a stop sign. Take advantage of the fact that your motorcycle has unlimited visibility, which can be turned into a big benefit at a stop sign.

Keeping Your Distance

—Just as a motorist must be aware of keeping his distance, so must a motorcyclist keep in mind his proximity to the car or cycle ahead. The chart printed below shows the safe stopping distance for cyclists—a set of numbers that every two-wheeled enthusiast should memorize for his safety and protection.

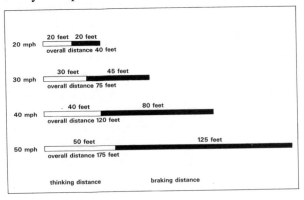

How to Pass

—Remember that when you are passing another vehicle—whether it be a two-wheeler or a car—make sure you pass *only* when you can see that the road ahead is clear. After you have passed, leave enough room to get back into your lane so that you don't "cut off" the vehicle you are passing. This is a simple piece of advice, but it is mighty important to both you and the fellow ahead.

Left-hand Turn

—Remember always, when you make a left-hand turn, to enter the left traffic lane well in advance of your turn—with a clear signal to those behind you that you are turning. This will give the vehicle behind you a chance to slow down and allow you to make the turn. Maintain a position in your traffic lane, which makes you visible in the rear view mirror of the cars in front of you. *Caution*—Be alert at all times for the motorist in your flow of traffic who may make a left-hand turn in front of you. Also look out for unsignaled turns in front of you from opposite lane traffic.

Sweeping a Curve

—If you're a professional racer, you follow certain rules when you sweep a raceway curve. Likewise, on a highway you also have rules to follow. Take your curves on the highway moderately, slowing down sufficiently so that you don't go into them with excess speed. (Excessive speed creates an increased centrifugal force, forcing your vehicle to the outside of a turn.) You will ride safer, and make a lot more friends if you follow this advice. And, of course, don't *ever* pass on a curve if someone is approaching in the other lane, or if the double highway line is in your lane.

U-Turns

—In areas where U-turns are allowed, remember this important point! Come to a complete stop, then look completely around to make sure that no one is coming. Take a second look! Then make your turn. This will avoid a lot of trouble, since you cannot take a chance that the road behind you is clear unless you check it out carefully.

Dress Neatly

—Along with your awareness of how to handle your motorcycle safely, comes also the responsibility you have to yourself, the AMA, the public, and your sport to present a neat appearance. Creating a better image is the personal responsibility of all cyclists. A safety helmet, clean leathers, or sports attire, the proper footwear, and an overall neat outfit can do a great deal to add to your acceptance and popularity. And when you dress neatly, you'll be paying tribute to yourself, your fellow riders and the AMA itself.

Your Goal

Whenever we talk about "two-wheeled wisdom," we are reminded of the message on the back of every AMA membership card. It is a statement by J. Edgar Hoover, famed director of the FBI. Here is what he has to say about "the most popular sport on wheels."

"The care you exercise in handling your vehicle will add to the safety of our streets and highways. It will also increase the pride and pleasure you take in an activity which, in many instances, is more than just a hobby."

This, then, is a brief lesson in "two-wheeled wisdom." We think you'll find that by following the suggestions, your riding will be not only more fun, but a lot more satisfying.

The AMA Helps All Riders

While the initials AMA means American Motorcycle Association, they can also be interpreted to mean Advancing Motorcycle Activities—because that is exactly what the AMA does for you as a rider when you "put your best wheel forward" and become a member.

The $2.00 annual fee you pay as a member of the AMA does many things. Here are just a few brief facts on what your membership brings:
- scheduling of thousands of fun-filled events such as scrambles, hill climbs, field meets, endurance runs, and race meets for you and your fellow riders. A major part of these events are such AMA services as—

a. classification of endurance riders, competition riders and hill climbers,
b. appointing referees and other officials,
c. direction of all races and other sanctioned events under standard rules,
d. awards for attendance at sanctioned tours,
e. record keeping of all events.

- a continuing public relations and educational program to make more people aware of the prestige and stature of your favorite sport through favorable magazine, newspaper, radio and television publicity.
- sanction of AMA clubs where you can enjoy meeting your fellow motorcyclists who share the same interest in a wholesome, healthful, thrilling sport.
- the advice and counsel of a 28-man Competition Committee of experts whose rulings are designed to provide fairness and equality in all phases of competition.
- the opportunity to subscribe to the magazine *American Motorcycling*—the official publication of the AMA—for $3.00 a year.
- an official AMA pin and membership card.

These are just a few of the many benefits you derive from joining the AMA — a membership that costs you less than four cents a week!!!! We think you'll agree that this is little enough to belong to the great fraternity of motorcyclists who share a common interest in "The greatest sport on wheels," and who enjoy countless hours of wholesome fun in one of the most thrilling of all sports.

In return for what the AMA does for you, the AMA member is asked to ride safely, dress neatly and set an example of conduct that will bring continued credit to his sport and the community he represents.

There are many ways an AMA member can show his fellow citizens that motorcycling "has come of age." Through membership in an official AMA club, members can take part in civic activities such as Civil Defense, blood donor programs, charity drives, courier service and similar projects.

Your conduct at rallies and other formal or informal events will go a long way in helping increase the stature of your sport among non-riders. The example you and your club members set will reflect upon the entire sport.

Remember, joining the AMA will put you in a group that is putting it "best wheel foward" to help strengthen the organization dedicated to Advancing Motorcycle Activities... *Your AMA*.

Here is what J. Edgar Hoover, famed head of the FBI, says about motorcycling:

"Simple courtesy is the key to acceptance, and motorcycle clubs, as well as individual owners, by adhering to a rigid code of courteous conduct, can do much to add to the safety of the highway."

*Ascot Park in
Gardena, California is one of the
finest dirt-track racing plants in
America. It also has a road racing
course and shown here is a group of
riders on one of the sharp dirt-track
corners. A.M.A. race promoter is
J. C. Agajanian of Indianapolis
racing fame.* (Below)

*Jumps like this are common and
enjoyed by the rider in a backwoods
contest.* (Opposite page)

In recent years motorcycles have been sold in large quantities for transportation and for highway and street use. In many instances the rider has no interest in sporting or competition events.

There are, however, many riders and dealers who feel that competition events of all kinds are most appealing to the rider, and the large number of competition events held throughout the world is evidence that this percentage of the business will continue to flourish and become even more popular. It is very popular these days to find many trailers, trucks and house trailers carrying small motorcycles en route to some vacation spot. It then thrills many riders to take the bikes and go into the backwoods country, the desert or the mountains because the trail bikes can reach isolated spots where the hunting and fishing are best and which territory no car can penetrate.

**by Bert W. Brundage
A.M.A. Competition Director,
District 37 Referee**

The inexperienced or uninformed rider is one of the most important problems facing professional motorcycle racing. Although people will argue "how can a rider get racing experience and know-how any other way except on the racetrack?," the facts prove that this is not the place to learn the ABC's of high speed competition.

It is a fairly simple operation to get a motorcycle, leathers and a Competition License, but the thing that is needed more than anything else, and by far the most difficult and expensive to obtain, is experience. This is a problem common to all apprentices in all professions.

There are four classes of riders now in racing,

Over rough terrain. (Far left)

A famous father and son team is Ed Kretz, Sr. and Jr. Ed, Sr. is a ten-time National A.M.A. Champion. Son, Eddie, has also won many championships. They are shown here testing a Swedish Lito competition bike for Cycle magazine. They are very successful motorcycle dealers in Monterey Park, California, handling Triumph, BMW, Honda and Suzuki.

many more in sporting events, but still the need for guided courses in track knowledge and methods is urgent. This does not necessarily mean lap after lap of practice under average conditions, because this is difficult to arrange insurance-wise and with race tracks.

By contrast, the race cars of today have a built-in factor which keeps many of the half-hearted racers out of competition. This is *money*, for only the determined have enough interest to keep trying to get a car to drive or to build one of their own. By the time either of these has been accomplished, the driver has been around the racing fraternity long enough to pick up the basic rules and do's and don't's. Also, very few race car owners will take a chance of having their equipment bent-up by a brand-new driver unless they are sure he can handle the car in a reasonably safe manner.

This untrained rider problem is not new and, therefore, attention must be given to all classes. There are a few amateur-class riders and some Experts who have not had enough track experience to really qualify for the classification they hold. The classification of a rider is sometimes due to the part of the country in which he earns his points. In areas where there is little competition, a rider can advance faster than in an area where there is hot competition and many events.

In most other sports that have both amateur and professional divisions, the contestant is usually among the best of the amateurs before he is even considered for the professional ranks. In motorcycling we have one of the best sporting groups or training grounds of any sport. The rider who earns his points or wins in sporting competition, scrambles, hare and hound, lightweight road races, etc., can handle himself in traffic or any emergency situation. Not only which lever to pull or pedal to push, but the ability to *think* of a one-shot decision that works is important.

One of the most important qualities of sporting competition is that it trains the rider to operate under pressure. When there are two bikes on your tail and one coming around the outside it's a different story to go fast and not fall off or lose control. I have noticed that most riders who come to flat track racing from the scrambles can handle a bike in an emergency and are good riders. Some don't like "C" racing and don't go real fast, but they are dependable.

A sportsman competition qualifying program would not be the answer for all areas, though, because there are not enough events. In any profession or sport, all is not learned in the field. In most cases the majority of learning time is spent in classes, group experiments, written tests or correspondence courses. This could apply to motorcycle racing as well. Pilots, truck drivers, even passenger car drivers have to pass a written test and an eye exam that are not easy. Stiffer requirements of this type, or training races, might lower the entries at race meets, but the riders who did make it would be first-class riders, safe for themselves and for the other riders.

The answer to these problems will not just *pop* out, but with effort, rigid qualifications and careful examination of facts, a system will be developed to make for more and better racing.

Through a tunnel in the desert.
(Left)

*For more than forty years motorcycle
racing at the Illinois State Fair at
Springfield has been an exciting
feature. The fifty-mile AMA National
Championship is held on the one-
mile dirt track each year.* (Bottom)

Sidecar racing looks dangerous but really isn't. The rider hangs far out on the corner to help keep the third wheel on the ground.

Sidecar motorcycle racing has always been more popular in Europe than in the United States, and sidecar events are scheduled for many important motorcycle racing programs—including the Isle of Man. (Left)

No luck came Gilera's way after a good start in the Spanish Grand Prix. Shortly after this T.T. shot was taken, Florian Canathias had to push the Gilera home to finish well down the field. The BMW monopoly seems unlikely to be broken for some time in the sidecar class. (Below)

Road racing at Cervia, Italy.

Kenny Weems in action at Corriganville, California. (Above)

Skip Van Leeuen, ace rider, in a TT event at El Cajon, California. (Above, right)

ISLE OF MAN T.T.—*Most famous
motorcycling event in the world is
the annual Isle of Man Tourist
Trophy races held on this small
island. Shown here are riders at
high speed over the winding roads
of this famous island. (Below and
right)*

*Motorcycle road racing in foreign
countries attracts thousands of spectators. This is the start of a road race
in England. Note the crowd on only
one of many corners. (Bottom)*

*Mud and water in the swamp fail to
detour this rough and ready
enthusiast. (Opposite page, top)*

Noted Los Angeles rider/dealer Bud Ekins gives helping hand to competitor/movie star Steve McQueen before start of California desert enduro.

Even Mini-Bike riders have fun says Ed Larson.

C. C. RYDER

"Sorry, Ed, the mustache has to go. Wind resistance, you know."

NUTS!

CROSS-COUNTRY RACE

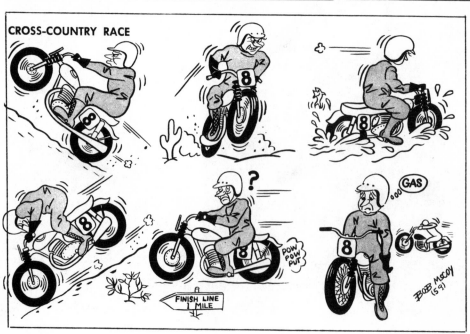

FINISH LINE 1 MILE

GAS

BOB McCOY ('59)

Start of a Desert Race over sand and sagebrush. (Opposite top)

Action is what riders like. (Opposite bottom)

Many riders enjoy riding a rear wheel. Doing a "wheelie" is fun.

In Canada road racing is popular. This shot is of the Canadian Motorcycle Championship held on Westwood Racing Circuit near Vancouver, B.C.

The real enthusiast, such as Bob Hicks, enjoys riding even in the mud and rain, plastered from helmet to toes, but he still has a happy smile on his face in this New England competition event. (Left)

A young contestant in the Mojave Desert of California.

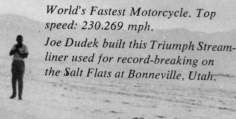

World's Fastest Motorcycle. Top speed: 230.269 mph.

Joe Dudek built this Triumph Stream-liner used for record-breaking on the Salt Flats at Bonneville, Utah.

VC 250

VC 883

racing revisions and show pieces

In 1964 Roger Reiman established new national and world's records for a 250cc displacement bike. He rode a Harley-Davidson Sprint. His speed was 156.24 mph.

Photo below shows the 55 cu. in. Harley-Davidson Sportster, which attained a speed of 178.26 mph.

What a combination! Californian have always been noted for strang combinations, and this one is no exception. It shows a Twin Honda engine mounted on a Mustang chassis. Even so, it has a Honda headlight. (Left)

Dan Sheppard is a man of imagina tion. He purchased an old police Harley-Davidson three-wheeler an gave it the "rickshaw" treatment. Note the classic carriage taillight. It has a folding top, and comfortab upholstered rear seat for two. (Far left)

A Vincent dragster in England.

*"The Quiet Kid"—a unique bike.
It has a homemade frame,
and the engine is a Scott-Atwater.
This bike did 145 mph at the
Bonneville Salt Flats in Utah. The
wheelbase was lengthened to enable
the installation of the unique engine.
Note that there are no foot pegs,
and the operator lies in a prone position, with his foot trailing behind the
rear wheel. (Below and bottom)*

A supercharged British dragster.

Motorcycle drag racing is extremely popular, and this 40-inch Triumph Twin is an example of a potent dragster. The bike was named by Rich Richards for his daughter Pam. He is recognized as an expert tuner, and his bikes have been responsible for many winners at the events at Bonneville and drag events. (Below, left)

A special double overhead cam bike at Bonneville, Utah, named "Double Trouble." (Below right)

Dragster with double twin engines. (Bottom)

This tiny motorcycle R&J Moore have often displayed at exhibitions in California. It certainly is one of the smallest operable motorcycles in the U.S. The wrenches in the foreground give an idea of the small size of the bike, but you can disregard Triumph nameplate, as it is a large 2-cycle engine. (Right)

"IT"

"IT" ...TO OUR KNOWLEDGE IS
THE SMALLEST MOTORCYCLE
THAT RUNS AND CAN BE RIDDEN
"IT" ...IS ALL HAND MADE TO SCALE
"IT" ...WILL RUN 45 M.P.H.
"IT" ...BELONGS TO R.&J. MOORE

Customized street models interest
many people, especially if they have
lots of chrome and special paint jobs.
Some have high handlebars which
most experienced riders consider
"freakish," and not suitable for use
in any kind of competition. This
early Triumph has a spring hub.

TWIN-ENGINE BSA DOES 140 MPH—
A special BSA which is the fastest
motorcycle dragster in Canada
powered by two BSA twin engines.
The owner, Richard Forest, of
Montreal, has turned 140 miles-per-
hour-plus in 1/4 mile stretch.

107

Almost hidden is this Harley-Davidson engine with this unusually heavy treatment of chrome. There is plenty of sparkle to this bike with twin carburetors. It is indeed a unique showpiece.

The diagrams on this page illustrate two different courses used at Daytona Beach. At top is the 3.1-mile circuit as used by the U.S.M.C. (F.I.M.) riders; and below is the 3.8-mile course used by the A.M.A. riders. Both circuits include flat portions of the road racing course, as well as sections of the high-speed banked raceway.

The largest, fastest and most famous speedway in the world, at Daytona Beach, Florida, is run by Bill France, who is also President of NASCAR, the stock car racing association. Shown here are many typical scenes at the annual Daytona Beach motorcycle races.

RACING AT DAYTONA BEACH, FLORIDA

Daytona Beach has long been the center of speed activities for cars and motorcycles. The finest racing plant in the United States is the International Speedway. President Bill France is a former motorcyclist and always schedules motorcycle events each year as a part of his speed program. Shown here is a map of the course used for the AMA events, although Mr. France also offers a program of FIM events sponsored by the USMC.

The Daytona 200

For 28 years, or ever since its first running in 1937, the Daytona 200 has been America's longest, richest, most important, and most challenging motorcycle race.

Over the years all of this country's top riders have fought for victory in the AMA's long test of skill, speed and endurance, first on the sands of the beach course, and in recent years over the silk-smooth asphalt of the Daytona International Speedway's 3.81-mile track and road layout.

First winner of the Daytona 200, back in 1937, was Ed Kretz, Sr., of Monterey Park, California, on an Indian, and at an average speed of 73.34 mph. The 22 winners since the Californian's

triumph include such racing greats as Ben Campanale, Babe Tancrede, Floyd Emde, Dick Klamfoth, Paul Goldsmith, Brad Andres, Joe Leonard, Don Burnett, Ralph White and Roger Reiman.

The record for the Daytona 200 was set in 1958 by Leonard when he streaked over the sands for a winning average of 99.86 mph.

The defending champion, Roger Reiman, who won in 1964 with a speed of 94.833 mph, used the 101 points that the Daytona 200 carries as the springboard that carried him to the AMA's Grand National Championship. No other race on the AMA calendar is so rich in points, so important to the man who has his sights set on the national title and the right to wear the big No. 1 on his racing machine.

Save for the World War II years—1942-46—the Daytona 200 has raced without a break. The beach course, with the Atlantic Ocean as a backdrop, was the site until 1961 when the men and machines moved to the recently completed International Speedway. At the Speedway, with its

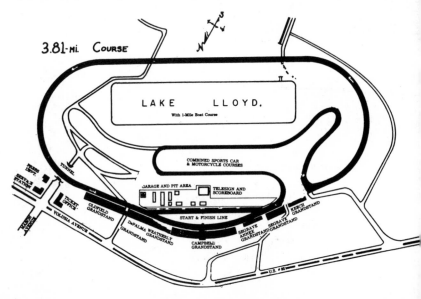

Three is company, five is a crowd—
at Daytona road race.

Piet Nortier of F.I.M. (in light suit)
shakes hands with Tom Galen,
USMC President. Standing next to
Galen is historian and Museum of
Speed owner, Bill Tuthill. At right
is Major Goode of F.I.M. Taken
during the USMC-F.I.M. races
at Daytona.

long, fast, straight, high-banked turns, and winding infield course, the riders were guaranteed an always perfect surface. No longer were they at the mercy of the tides and wind.

There are few more thrilling sights in sports than that of a Daytona 200 field, numbering close to 100 powerful motorcycles, in action on the Speedway's 3.81-mile course. There are flat-out speeds on the straights and banks. There is breath-stopping traffic on the turns in the winding infield road. It is a race that offers no respite to bike or rider.

It is, in short, America's finest two-wheel show.

USMC World Championship Races

No other sports event in the United States each year brings together such a collection of world champions as does the USMC International meet at Daytona International Speedway.

In 1964 champion motorcycle riders from five continents and thirteen countries competed in four events in four classes. These are the only races in America which are on the FIM calendar and which carry points leading to world titles.

In the four classes and four races, which ranged in length from 60 to 200 kilometers, the international champions displayed 21 different makes of the world's fastest racing motorcycles. These super-performance bikes included the MV Agusta, world's fastest and costliest, Suzuki, Kreidler, Ducati, Honda, Yamaha, Bultaco, Greeves, Tohatsu, MZ, Parilla, Benelli, Aermacchi, Matchless, Norton, BMW, Gilera, and A.J.S.

George Talcott slides down a hill in Alligator Enduro, part of Daytona Motorcycle Week program. (Left)

Down he goes.

Mechanic from Japan tunes a Daytona Yamaha.

The start of a championship race at Daytona Speedway.

Down he goes.

Miss BSA (Holly Wertham)—taken at Daytona Beach speed classic. Machine is a Lightning model.

A fiberglass fairing comes "unglued" in a spill. (Left)
Acrobatics—Even though a spill like this one looks dangerous, it usually isn't. (Below)
Peggy Ann Dovel on a Harley-Davidson competes in the Alligator Classic at Daytona Beach. Her husband, Darrell, is a dirt track and road-racing expert. (Bottom)

The continents represented in the world point meet were Australia, Asia, Europe, Africa, and North and South America, and the countries included Japan, Germany, France, United States, Canada, England, Italy, Switzerland, Argentina, Holland, New Zealand, Austria, and South Africa.

The USMC riders compete over the Speedway's exceptionally fast 3.1-mile course, which combines a long straight and one banked turn of the Speedway proper, with the winding infield road.

The four classes of machines raced are 50cc, 125cc, 250cc, and 500cc, and they race at 60, 100, 125, and 200 kilometers, respectively.

The USMC riders include most of the men who, in their European meetings, regularly draw crowds of 250,000 and up. Such world-famed champs as Mike Hailwood, Hugh Anderson, Mitsuo Itoh, Jean Pierre Beltoise, Alan Shepherd, Tarquinio Provini, Phil Read, and Benedicto Caldarella, all have shown their speed and daring on the Speedway's international course.

It was on the Speedway's full 2.5-mile automobile course that Hailwood of England, riding an MV Agusta, last year established a world mark for one hour of racing. Hailwood covered 233.081 kilometers at an average speed of 144.829 mph.

When one has seen the annual Daytona Motorcycle Classics, with its riders from USMC and AMA, one has seen the best that the world has to offer in the sport.

Norman Bergquist hits the grass.

A near hit!

Fun on asphalt!

Hey—Hey—What am I doing here
—blocking traffic?

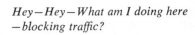

Excessive exhaust smoking means
there's something wrong.

There were many unique bikes
competing in the first British Drag
Festival including one very long
two-wheeler using a Volkswagen
engine. (Top)

Volkswagen powered dragster.
(Center)

Don Hyland—twin RNG Parasite Tri.

WORLD'S ROAD RACING CHAMPION-
HAILWOOD. *Mike Hailwood of
England has for some years past been
the outstanding road-racing champion of the world under F.I.M. rules.
Young Mike, the son of the largest
motorcycle dealer in the world who
operates about 15 motorcycle sales
agencies throughout England, is
living proof of what an ambitious
and skillful young man can do with
a motorcycle. Young Mike is a
millionaire in his own name and
rides fast racing motorcycles for the
sport of it and not because he needs
the money. Shown* (Right) *are Mike
and his father with many of his
beautiful racing trophies won in
contests in which he has competed*

*the young millionaire
world's champion —
mike hailwood*

throughout the world. While Mike is a skilled road rider and certainly one of the best the world has ever known, he does not compete on American type flat-tracks, nor has he ever competed under an American Mortocycle Association sanction. This is because the F.I.M., which governs international motorcycle racing is not affiliated with the American Motorcycle Association which sanctions motorcycle competition in the United States.

Champion Hailwood in action on a 4-cylinder Italian MV-Agusta, on which he won many races. (Left)

Hailwood at Daytona Beach F.I.M. (U.S.M.C.) races. (Below)

Hailwood wins trophy at Daytona Beach after his world's (F.I.M.) circular-track record.

When John Penton broke the trans-continental record on a BMW, he was the honored guest at Ascot Speedway the evening he finished his record run. He was the guest of J. C. Agajanian, promoter of the race. Penton is shaking hands with the famed Indianapolis driver Rodger Ward and the then Mrs. Ward.

In 1959, John Penton of Lorain, Ohio, established a coast-to-coast motorcycle record of 52 hours, 11 minutes from New York City to Los Angeles. His time was checked by Western Union and his record has never been beaten. Penton rode a BMW R-69 model. He has won many endurance championships including the famous Jack Pine Enduro in Michigan. At the time of the record Penton was thirty-three years old, a physical culture instructor with tremendous endurance and great ability as a motorcyclist who can ride long hours without fatigue. He took only three hours out for sleeping during the long record-breaking grind. When asked why he undertook such a strenuous journey, he replied, "Just for kicks." Photo shows Penton checking in at the Western Union office in Los Angeles, California, after breaking the 20-year-old former record of 76 hours. Shown in the other photo is a close-up of Penton taken the day after he finished being interviewed by *Cycle* magazine publisher, Floyd Clymer, and at left, Earl Flanders of Pasadena, California, BMW Western Distributor.

Twenty-six-year-old Craig Breedlove is the owner and driver of the three-wheel jet car titled "Spirit of America." Sponsored by the Shell Oil Company and the Goodyear Tire and Rubber Company, Breedlove set a new world's straight-away speed record at Bonneville, Utah, and first to break the 500 mile an hour barrier. Being a three-wheeled vehicle, it was recognized by the F.I.M. as a motorcycle. Breedlove is the world's fastest motorcyclist. Breedlove and his wife, also shown in the photos, riding Yamahas, are both enthusiastic motorcyclists.

Each weekend and during vacation times thousands of motorcyclists gather in every state to enjoy the sport of motorcycling and the great outdoors and to have fun.

On the following page, a group of enthusiasts thoroughly enjoy competing over a sandhill. It looks dangerous but it really isn't. Most competition riders wear leathers for protection while racing in competition events.

Many riders enjoy traveling over hilly, sandy terrain. It is tough on men and machines, and this kind of action separates the men from the boys—although the boys sometimes win!

Neufeld Carry—It carries bike up to 300 lbs. (Right)

The powerful, heavy Harley-Davidson "74" is ideally suited to long-distance travel at highway cruising speeds, under a full load of camping gear plus rider and passenger. (Below, left and right)

One of the many Shriners' Drill Teams using motorcycles at the recent Shriners' Convention in New York City. (Bottom)

Internationally-known bandleader, Don Ricardo, likes competitive events; is leading light of BMW Owner's Club.

Small group outings by motorcycle have an unmatched friendliness. Typical is this relaxed BMW owners' club run. (Right)

An attractive young Danish girl enjoys scootering. Shown alongside Copenhagen's little mermaid in the harbor.

The Commando Motorcycle Display Squad of England rides Triumphs in their unique exhibitions. They are on world tour.

Road tests are popular and used extensively in motorcycle magazines. Shown here is Lyn Abrams, Editor of Cycle magazine, making a jump on a Spanish Montesa Diablo. It's fun to be "airborne." (Left)

Cyclists can always have fun in a contest to show their skill in winding in and out and between traffic markers at the Honda Fun Festival.

Many riders have fun in the sand, or on short steep hills. Sometimes the bikes rear up on the rear wheel—looks dangerous, but really isn't.

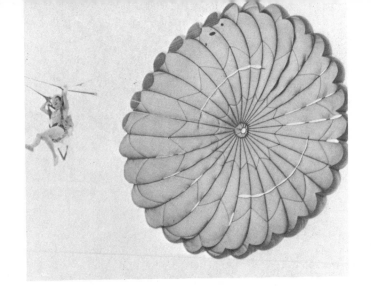

PARA-KITING

Para-kiting is an interesting although somewhat dangerous game that intrigues only the most adventurous enthusiasts. The rider is towed into the air by a motorcycle and later disconnects the rope from the cycle and parachutes to earth. For those who do not like such an exciting sport, there are many other interesting games that motorcycle riders enjoy to the utmost, such as: polo, ride-the-plank, teeter-tottering, tug-o-war, spark plug changing contests, egg and sack races, push a machine race, ditto, push a machine backward race, economy contests and many other interesting games.

The sport of Para-kiting started in France. It is America's newest and fast-booming sport, according to writer John Pitts and photographer John Gregoire.

Joan Howe, former Suzuki Company employee, now of Disneyland Convention Sales, receives riding instructions from former competition star, one-time National Champion and now Suzuki Sales Manager Walt Fulton. (Left)

Action in a California Scrambles event. (Center)

When home, the author of this book takes a short motorcycle ride every night, weather permitting, for fun and health. However, Clymer's four-year-old Afghan hound, Shara, can hardly wait to enjoy an eight-block spin running alongside the bike. Shara, who gets all of the exercise, is even more enthusiastic about cycles than her owner. Bike is a French Mobylette. (Bottom)

One of most popular motorcycle events in Southern California is a comparative newcomer to the scene—and all indications are that the William E. Johnson Invitational will continue to grow each year as an event that combines the competitive aspect with the relaxation of a scenic tour through the mountains. The event takes the form of a rally complete with checkpoints and time schedules.

Winners are chosen on the basis of fewest points lost at checkpoints. Riders come from far and near with every make and model machine. This year, the second annual event, there were close to 400 entrants in all classes. Following the all day run, participants were treated to a delicious buffet banquet complete with winners' awards, doorprizes, and entertainment. Many motorcycling dignitaries were present including visiting officials from England, representing the Triumph organization.

The event is sponsored by Western United States Triumph distributors Johnson Motors Inc., of Pasadena, California, in honor of the late William E. Johnson, pioneer British motorcycle distributor and beloved sportsman.

Emphasis is placed on neat appearance, and it was generally agreed that those participating were a symbol of proper motorcycling. Overall winners, with only four points lost, were Ronald and Felicia Monday. Runnerup was enduro champ Cal Brown.

Chairman of the event was then Johnson Motors Sales Mgr. Don Brown. Dealers Norm Lee and Hazen Blair were in charge of routing. Pete Colman took care of the timing equipment and Buck Smith tallied the score cards. Honorary starter was AMA Executive Secretary Lin Kuchler.

French humor. (Right)

Riders pause to relax and chat before start of annual Johnson Invitational.

This cyclist wears a lightweight rubberized rainproof garment over a business suit. The hood, safety helmet and face shield enable this rider to keep relatively dry in wet weather. This equipment is fine for many business men who are now riding motorcycles to and from work due to congestion and parking problems in most cities. (Below)

Publicity-minded U.S. Suzuki Vice-President Jack McCormack. He is being interviewed on the "Story Line" CBS show with producer-M.C. Dennis Bracken with back to the camera. McCormack not only had a Suzuki in the studio, but spent an hour answering questions and talking about the fun of cycling. (Bottom)

Many sportsmen, like this Triumph Cub rider, like to follow the good fishing streams or seek out hunting grounds which can be easily reached by riding off-road trails in the back country.

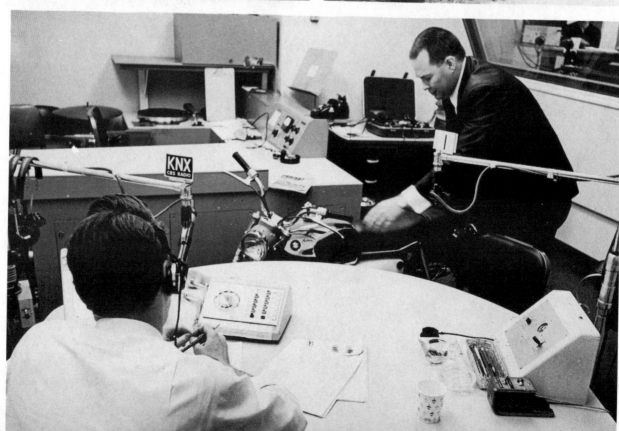

"Tell us more about your motorcycle trip."

— THE SATURDAY EVENING POST

Going by motorcycle is now more popular than ever and many individual riders as well as riders in groups have found fun and satisfaction in cross country traveling. Many of these adventuresome individuals like to camp out in the open. Therefore, the following article by Cliff Boswell, who has for many years been the travel authority and correspondent for *Cycle* magazine is included. No one is more qualified to write on travel and camping than Mr. Boswell, who is a school teacher by profession and an enthusiastic motorcyclist by choice.

MOTORCYCLE TRAVEL AND EQUIPMENT

by Cliff Boswell

From the Arctic Circle to the tip of South America no road or by-way escapes the adventurous motorcyclist in his restless quest for new places, and his consuming desire for riding long and far. At least one rider completed the entire journey from Alaska to the Strait of Magellan, and two more were headed that way at this writing.

Roads through Mexico to Central America, the Alcan and Trans-Canada 1 are becoming known to the many cyclists forever stretching their travel horizons into lands north and south of the border. Even Europe and Africa are not too much out of the way for many avid motorcyclists bent upon sight-seeing away from home.

Within the boundaries of the U.S. the great transcontinental highways east and west and north and south see an increasing number of motorcyclists visiting the scenic and historical wonders of our own country, and sampling the network of side roads interlacing the land from coast to coast and border to border. Whether traveling alone with full camping equipment, or riding with a large group on a week-end trip, the motorcyclist is the most independent operator on the road. With a good machine to do his bidding, a bed roll on the back, he should not worry about how to get there or where to stay enroute.

Motorcycle traveling, however, brings its own peculiar problems which must be coped with if one is to remain safe and comfortable—it takes a certain amount of good judgment, alertness, sensitiveness to speed and road conditions, and perceptiveness not possessed by every driver of an automobile.

A cyclist must drive defensively at all times— eternally on the lookout for road hazards, for automobiles that may stop or turn in front of him or pull into him from a side-road. He must practice vigilance until it becomes a habit. He must learn to use the agility and maneuverability of his vehicle to keep him out of trouble as well as to propel him along the road quickly and safely.

There is, of course, a difference between riding a high-speed touring machine designed for maintaining top road speeds and a small calibre bike engineered for off-road travel or for scooting down to the corner grocery store. Each one has its place, and, whereas the large capacity machine can be used for short hops as well as long ones, the small bike will be out of place in a traffic situation where speed and power are necessary. In

Boswell and motorcycle outfitted for a long trip. Note the tripod fastened on the side of the pack. It is enclosed in rubberized bags.

any condition the motorcycle should be fast enough to keep up with the normal traffic expected.

This is not to say, however, that lightweight machines have not been used for long-distance travel. Quite the contrary is true. Many small cc scooters and cycles have been driven for great distances where their lightness and low gasoline consumption have been advantageous. The author is acquainted with a young man who rode a scooter around the perimeter of Australia, for example.

Normally, though, a motorcycle can safely be ridden in the center of the right-hand lane of traffic—too close to the center stripe encourages wild drivers to pass on the right, while too close to the outside edge will tempt them to force him onto the shoulder. This position affords the rider an opportunity to quickly maneuver right or left in an emergency.

Hand signals should be used, even exaggerated, when moving from one lane to another, when passing, stopping or slowing down. The small size of a cycle as compared with an automobile or truck makes the use of hand signals especially important.

Road hazards include such obstructions as mud, gravel, rocks and puddles of water or running water on or across the highway. Thunderstorms can bring all of these hazards to desert or mountain travelers. Snow and ice are to be watched for, too, on certain occasions.

Riding in large groups brings its own set of rules. Some of the riding clubs now organize their members into groups of four with a leader and cut-off man assigned to each group. Riders are staggered to avoid colliding with one another and hand signals are strictly observed with each group riding and moving as a unit. The BMW Club of Southern California has experimented at length with safe group-riding methods, and furnishes printed rules to each member. Other large groups have done likewise. Some clubs ride in uniform to tour events.

Aside from a common-sense set of road rules it must be recognized that certain other conditions are present in motorcycle riding which are not common to automobile travel. We might say that motorcycling is more akin to hiking or horseback riding where no built-in protection against the weather is found. Regardless of some of the new windscreens and touring fairings available, the cycle rider is only partially protected from rain, wind and cold and not at all from the sun. But, part of the fun of this sport is to pick up the gauntlet, and fight back. The capriciousness of weather, at any time of the year offers a challenge that can best be faced in a spirit of good sportsmanship where preparation for any eventuality short of tornado or earthquake must be made in advance.

Answers are to be found in special clothing and practical accessories which give reasonable protection yet do not restrict the actions of the rider or hamper the handling of the motorcycle.

Some riders prefer no wind protection device at all; others like a full touring fairing for maximum weather protection. In between lie many

Sightseeing the famous Franciscan Missions in California is a popular pastime of many motorcyclists. This is San Luis Rey north of San Diego.

Boswell enjoys touring with many different makes for his articles in CYCLE Magazine. Shown here is a Triumph fully packed for touring, and a Harley-Davidson in the Mojave Desert with the cactus in the background.

135

Cooking utensils to be carried on a motorcycle trip should include can opener, on right, and a canteen, as well as extra gasoline for the stove.

variations. I feel that in the long run a rider will be less wearied and wind-burned if some kind of windshield is used.

The streamlined jobs are best, as they give better hand and arm protection, run better into the wind, and are stronger than the handlebar-mounted models popular a short time back. My personal preference is for a two-piece fairing which permits the removal of the lower part in hot weather.

The single-piece fairing offers some advantages over the two-piece, but the flexibility of the latter makes it my choice for year-round riding.

Now the question of riding apparel. This country is finally beginning to manufacture adequate clothing for the motorcycle rider. U.S. manufacturers have made very fine leather jackets and trousers for years as well as good leather gloves and riding boots, but very little was done in the way of rain clothes, shirts and light trousers. Probably the best helmets are made in this country, although this is a fairly recent innovation to motorcycling. At least one large motorcycle manufacturer in the U.S. now markets a very acceptable range of clothing.

Basically, clothing must be chosen which will keep a rider dry in wet weather, warm in cold weather, and cool in hot weather. It must fit snugly enough not to flap—this applies to shirts and pants, specifically. Rain clothes must be heavy enough to withstand continuous pelting of driving rain for several hours at a time, and must fit snugly at ankles, wrists and neck. Light neoprene suits are incapable of withstanding this

kind of treatment. Rubberized cotton or nylon are best. Single piece as well as two-piece suits are available.

Boots can be insulated or not. They should be high enough to protect the ankles and to extend inside the pants cuff far enough that wind does not get between. Some are laced; some are slip-over.

Light colored pants are best worn in hot weather, with woolen or leather being suitable for cold spells. Leather is a natural for motorcycling garments as it is warm, gives good wind protection, does not flap and is porous enough to permit some air circulation. Leather garments should be lined for best protection and for easy removal.

Shirts, if worn without jackets should fit snugly. A flapping shirt collar or sleeve can be very annoying beside causing a sore spot on throat or arm.

My preference is for several layers of fairly light clothes that may be donned or removed piece by piece as weather or riding conditions demand. Insulated underwear can be carried for special occasions, and light jackets of wool or cotton are handy. Naugahyde jackets are warm, but may cause sweating.

Goggles or a visor should be carried even with a windshield, and a light pair of gloves as well as a heavy pair are necessary. Of course, no outfit is complete without a good helmet. A white helmet is best for hot weather to protect against sunstroke. It is easily seen at night, and in this respect gives added protection.

Camping and traveling gear laid out ready to be loaded.

Large panniers and rear luggage carrying cases on Harley-Davidsons.

Motorcyclists are individualists and they are ingenious. These traits show up in the many modified machines seen on the road, and in the do-it-yourself attitude in building accessories to fit different needs. Rear fender racks for toting camping gear are as varied as the several owners' inventiveness can make them, and they run from strictly utilitarian jobs whomped up at the last minute to ornate devices built to enhance the design of the machine.

Much of a rider's duffle is carried in saddle bags or "panniers" as per the newest term. Leather and canvas bags have largely been replaced by plastic or fiberglass panniers in recent years, as they furnish better weather protection and more style. They can be locked, and some are removable for transporting into a room at night. Although homemade panniers are common, most riders find it more convenient to purchase a good set and adapt them to their particular machine. U.S. manufacturers have made some fine contributions to the field of motorcycle accessories. Some outstanding examples of tooled leather saddlebags, however, show up at disconcerting intervals to refute this trend.

Large, removable boxes carried on the rear luggage rack are popular on some of the large machines, and two "campers" patterned after the prevalent truck-camper outfits were seen at the 1965 Death Valley Run. These outfits are large enough to carry a gasoline stove, bed rolls or sleeping bags, and food and clothing for one or two riders.

A unique, lightweight tent designed for use of motorcyclists is the "Pop-Tent Camper" which sleeps two in its seven-foot enclosure. Fiberglass ribs provide the only support needed while sewn-in ground cloth and mosquito netting provide complete protection. A storm flap can be extended to make a sheltered entrance.

Another exciting innovation of the inventive motorcycle rider is the small motorcycle-towed trailer. Most of them, so far, have been of the two-wheel variety, although one or two single-wheel jobs have been observed. Where this trend will lead is difficult to say, but there is no doubt that several serious-minded individuals are working hard to develop a practical towing trailer for the large motorcycles.

Camping with a motorcycle is a sport enjoyed by large numbers of enthusiasts in this country. In no other manner, except by foot or horseback, can the traveler enjoy such complete independence from commercial establishments or such freedom of movement. He can stay just about where he pleases, he can sleep in the open or in a small shelter, he can cook his own meals, he can range far and wide, and he can do all these at a fraction of the cost of any other means of transportation. By utilizing roadside rest stops, Forest Service Camps, community parks and any part of the wide open spaces available in many sections of America, he can travel at less cost than staying at home.

The prospective motorcyclist-camper needs a few basic items of equipment which are essential to his happiness and well-being, however. They are: (1) a good lightweight tent—not a pup tent, (2) sleeping bag (3) air mattress (4) ground cloth (5) small gasoline stove (6) cooking and eating utensils (7) canteen. Beyond this list, items can be added to suit one's taste, but the deletion of any single piece mentioned will substantially lower the prospects for a full enjoyment of independence.

Along with a good tent, of course, goes the necessary equipment for setting it up. This can include tent pegs and support poles. My preference is for a lightweight waterproof tent with sewn-in waterproof ground cloth and with as few poles as possible. It must be adequately ventilated through screened windows or vents to prevent sweating, and it must be of sufficient height to at least permit the occupant to sit upright. It should be easily erected, and it should have mosquito netting over the door with a "fly" extending above the door. Several tents are available which meet these specifications.

A waterproof ground cloth is necessary when sleeping in the open on the ground. It prevents moisture from entering the sleeping bag, and gives protection to clothing from ground moisture. If much camping is expected without use of a tent, a second ground cloth of light waterproof canvas or plastic is ideal for covering extra equipment and clothing at night. For the greatest comfort clothing should be removed at night.

Sleeping is no problem if a good rubberized air mattress is used under a sleeping bag. One may have to sacrifice a few precious pounds of weight in carrying a good mattress and a warm bag, but it is worth it. Plastic air mattresses are not as satisfactory as rubber impregnated nylon or cotton.

One's size will determine the width and length of his sleeping bag. I prefer a down bag because it can be rolled into a compact bundle, because it is light in weight, and possesses a wide temperature range for comfort. But, innumerable sleeping bags are available to suit any person's pocket

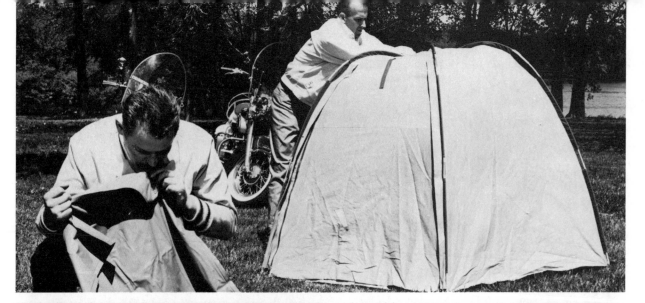

book and desires. Down and feather bags can often be located in war surplus stores at very reasonable prices.

Cooking utensils will usually include a frying pan (a small cast iron pan is best), small kettle or No. 10 can, and perhaps a second small pan with bail. Eating utensils will include a cup (plastic preferred) knife-fork-spoon combo, large spoon, plate. A few basic necessities such as dish washing detergent, a scouring pad, powdered coffee or tea, sugar, powdered cream, salt, pepper, and cooking oil can be carried regularly, but basic foods are easily purchased from day to day as needed. With the large variety of canned and dried foods available from any modern grocery store there is little need to carry them on a trip.

Several compact stoves are available for the motorcyclist-camper with the Swedish Primus stove being the smallest one capable of producing adequate heat for desired purposes. The one-quart size G. I. stove is OK as well as a single-burner stove utilizing bottled gas. The latter is somewhat bulky, and extra cans of Butane may not be available. Another Swedish stove, the Optimus, is available at some stores in single and double burner sizes.

Alcohol burning stoves do not appear to be as satisfactory mainly because of the difficulty of finding fuel.

The following 5-day menu was used on a motorcycle trip to the Mojave Desert with all food being purchased at the start. It is usually not necessary to carry all ingredients unless the trip involves a prolonged stay in a remote area.

There are many fine foods available for the motorcycle traveler.

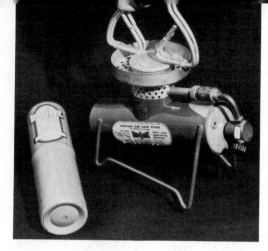

An excellent portable stove—Bernz-O-Matic.

	Breakfast	Lunch	Supper
1st day	sausage	boiled egg	beef hash
	eggs	banana	asparagus
	orange	boullion cube	bread
	bread	crackers	coffee
	coffee	tea or milk	cookies
2nd day	orange	dehydrated soup	spaghetti & meat
	rolled oats	cheese	instant pudding
	with raisins	crackers	peas
	sausage	tea or milk	coffee
			bread
			dried prunes
3rd day	bacon	bouillon cube	macaroni-cheese
	eggs	apple	beans
	prunes	boiled egg	canned peaches
	bread	tea or milk	bread
	coffee		cookies
			coffee
4th day	canned peaches	spam	beef hash
	dry cereal	apple	canned corn
	bacon	crackers	Boston brown bread
	milk for cereal	bouillon cube	canned apricots
	coffee	tea or milk	coffee
5th day	canned apricots	Boston bread	beef stew
	rolled oats		canned tomatoes
	spam	dehydrated soup	instant pudding
	coffee	cheese	bread
		tea or milk	coffee

Note: concentrated lemon juice may be carried instead of bulk oranges, or lemon powder is good. Try the small soup cracker instead of the large soda cracker that breaks up so easily. Supper and breakfast are usually eaten at the same place; so, some items may be held over from one meal to the other, i.e., cook prunes for supper, and save some for breakfast.

Riders descending into the Panamint Valley north of Trona. The Panamint Range in the distance. The Panamint Valley is about 1000 feet higher in elevation than Death Valley and almost as large. (Below)

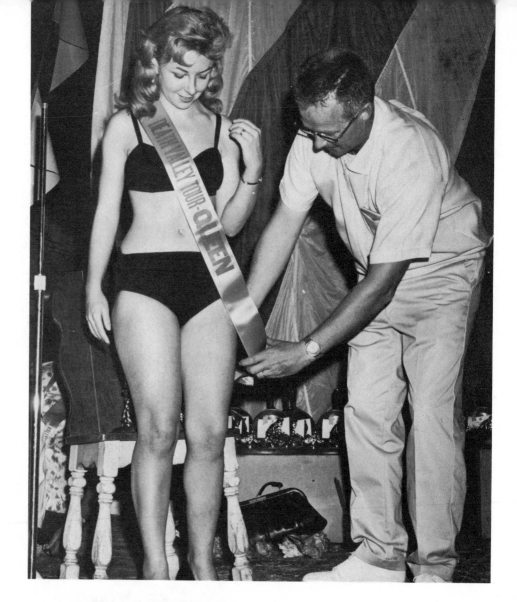

The Death Valley Tour Queen receives her ribbon from Dick Hutchins, spark plug of the Tour.

Now 8% of cycle riders are estimated to be women, as it's easy to learn to ride. (left)

Neatly attached luggage and streamlined saddle bags enable the traveler to carry every necessity.

Many travelers carry fancy traveling bags, as shown here.

A neat cellophane enclosure keeps maps dry.

In contrast with the hot Mojave Desert of Death Valley, we find German and Dutch riders camping in a winter snow storm near Iserlohn, Germany. They wrote that those who were there will long remember the fun that they had.

The largest motorcycle tour in the world has been held for the past ten years and is known as the Death Valley Run. Last year more than 2,400 enthusiasts met in colorful Death Valley for a week-end of fun, sport and good fellowship.

HISTORY OF
THE DEATH VALLEY TOUR

by Cliff Boswell

The tenth annual Death Valley Run was celebrated last October when 2,400 registered motorcyclists plus an estimated 300 guests descended upon historic Furnace Creek Ranch for a week-end of fun and camping. From all points of the compass they came, from as far away as Seattle, Washington, from Idaho, Nevada, Oregon, Arizona and from all points in California. In ten years the Death Valley Run has developed into the greatest event of its kind in the world. The Washington 99er Motorcycle Club rode 1,200 miles as a group to the 10th anniversary event to win first place trophy for the longest distance traveled.

The first run in 1954 began inauspiciously enough with 200 riders, and little did its backers dream that in a few short years the lure of the Valley and the excitement of this gathering in one of the most remote areas of the U.S. would attract the greatest number of road riders on the continent.

It all started in 1953 when about a dozen motorcycle dealers, sports committeemen and enthusiasts got together in Los Angeles to talk about competition *and* road riding. Howard

Angel, then president of the Sports Committee and a road rider as well as a competition rider asked for a road event that would pull in a large number of riding enthusiasts. He contended, and others agreed, that competition was getting a disproportionate amount of attention, and that something should be done to give the people making up the majority of motorcycle purchasers an opportunity to participate in an event of their own.

Dick Hutchins, present sponsor of the Death Valley Run, and now partner with Len Russell in Harley-Davidson in Los Angeles, was present at the meeting, and suggested Death Valley as a possibility. The idea caught on, and the Death Valley Run was born. The last week-end in October, which coincides closely with the official opening of the Death Valley season, was chosen as best suited to a gathering of this nature. Fierce heats of summer would be gone by this date, and a minimum number of tourists would be expected.

The initial event was then scheduled for 1954 after additional meetings and planning, and the Jackass Enduro was included as an added attraction. This was a tough event beginning at Trona near the Panamint Valley and finishing at Texas Springs Camp in Death Valley. Its route lay through sand washes and rough canyons from the bed of mineral-rich Searles Lake through the Panamint Mountains to below sea level at Death Valley.

Road riders assembled at the fair ground in Lancaster on Friday night; then took a devious route by map to Trona, through Wildrose Canyon

The Lucky Wheels Club, all riding double, show their group riding techniques. Note the small lad on the tank of the Harley-Davidson on the left. (Top)

The Riding Roulettes from Las Vegas, Nevada, show off their two trailers as they enter the Furnace Creek Ranch headquarters. (Center)

A number of customized motorcycles parked at the Furnace Creek entrance, general meeting grounds for all riders. (Bottom)

and through the eastern entrance to the Valley. Check points were located at Red Mountain, Trona, Wildrose and Stovepipe Wells.

As I remember some of the early Runs, considerable rain fell, and washouts and some flooding made cautious riding necessary.

As the Death Valley Run grew year by year, the dual job of sponsoring it and the Jackass Enduro became too great; so the enduro was discontinued after four years.

The official starting point was changed from Lancaster to Victorville in 1959. A heavy rain, there, caused all persons to move inside a building at the fair ground, and it became obvious that with the large numbers of people involved, an official starting place would no longer be practical.

Consequent runs, therefore, saw riders converging upon Death Valley from two entrances, and finally from four. With no official starting time or place riders were now free to enter the nearest available route, but were required to come through between certain hours on Saturday in order to qualify for trophies.

In the early years of the Run all events were held at the Texas Springs campground in Death Valley. All motorcyclists slept there in the open or under canvas, the famous western feed donated by Southern California Harley-Davidson dealers was served there, and all judging and presentations of trophies were made there.

Later the event moved to the Furnace Creek Ranch and to a level campground behind the Death Valley National Monument Visitors

This young lady and her family are real motorcycle enthusiasts, and the big Harley-Davidson pulls their trailer on the tour.

Russ Good on his beautiful 1911 Excelsior and his early-day riders costume brought him first place. Machines have to be ridden in from the nearest check point—about 20 miles.

Center. At the present time, all activities are held on the parking lot and lawns of the Furnace Creek Ranch. The Death Valley Committee reserves a block of motel rooms convenient to the activities area, and cyclists occupy the rest of the motel area or the campgrounds.

The popularity of the Run can be laid to its organization, to the nature of the tour and to its location. No single factor can entirely account for its growth.

This is a road rider's event. No doubt of it. No contests of any kind except those directly connected with road riding are staged. Riders respond to this concept by readying their machines, preparing good equipment and bringing the whole family, or as much of it as possible. With the average distance being about 300 miles one way, and practically all of it across broad expanses of desert, it is a challenge to any motorcyclist traveler.

Riders may expect to encounter anything from warm weather in the lowlands to high winds and even snow flurries in the mountain passes, and they must prepare accordingly. Most of them carry camping equipment including small tents and sleeping bags, and cooking equipment.

Many couples ride double with their duffle fastened to the rear luggage rack and carried in saddle bags, while others ride separate machines with the husband on one and wife on another. Whole families including small children show up also. It is not uncommon to find mama with a daughter riding double behind her and papa with a son on the rear seat. One family came with two

146

Members of the famous Victor McLaglen Motorcycle Corps start Saturday evening's festivities with some fancy riding.

large motorcycles, each with a side car. Another built a small seat for their young son fitted to the gasoline tank. A few, even, bring their pets in specially constructed dog houses, or riding on a pad on the tank. If close to 3,000 motorcycles arrive we can estimate that at least 4,000 people are on them.

All kinds of fascinating equipment show up, the latest of which were two small teardrop trailers towed by members of the Las Vegas Motorcycle Club.

The organization of the Death Valley Run remains similar from year to year with the same events eagerly anticipated. One of the original contests is a flapjack cooking contest in which couples are furnished a small frying pan, a bundle of kindling, matches, water and pancake mix. At the starting signal the man gets a fire going while the woman mixes the pancake batter and pours it into the pan. Then the husband cooks it, and finally feeds it to his wife. First couple finished wins a coveted Death Valley award consisting of a small iron frying pan mounted on a wooden base behind a small statue of a prospector and a motorcycle rider. This trophy was modified in 1964 because of the difficulty of obtaining it in its original form. A small frying-pan pin engraved with the Death Valley Tour and the date is given to each participant. Both trophy and pin were derived from the flapjack cooking contest.

Other contests include the popular Death Valley Tour Queen event, the rider with the baldest head, the fattest rider, shortest, tallest, best dressed couple, best man solo, best woman solo, best modified machine, best side car, best family, best looking club, oldest machine ridden to the event, rider traveling the greatest distance, club traveling the farthest, youngest rider, best looking legs (men only). In addition 15 gold rush trophies are drawn by lot, a sweepstakes trophy is awarded and the first and second to register are presented awards.

Because of the large number of contestants in 1965, trophies were awarded to custom and stock classes of motorcycles in four categories, and several sub-classes were added to include motorcycles of similar sizes.

Dick Hutchins, who sponsors the event, acts as master of ceremonies. He is assisted by Death Valley Committee co-chairman, Ed Anderson. A group of about 25 dealers, their wives, and other motorcyclists make up a Death Valley Committee which takes care of the multitudinous tasks involved in running and supervising an event of this size.

The annual Saturday afternoon western feed, free to all registered riders, is furnished by donations from Harley-Davidson Dealers in Southern California. Up until last year it was served by dealers and their wives, but its preparation and serving is now done by Fred Harvey Enterprises, owners of Furnace Creek Ranch. Saturday evening's activities begin with a flag salute and stunt riding by the Victor McLaglen Motorcycle Corps of Los Angeles. Contests then follow in rapid succession. Sunday morning includes judging for best dressed couples, singles and machines. Riders depart for home about noon.

Bruce and Linda Chubbuck show off one of the unusual Death Valley Run trophies.

No rowdy element has ever been allowed to interrupt the Death Valley Run or any of its events because of the alertness and cooperation of law enforcement agencies from the state, county and the National Monument. The California Highway Patrol, the Inyo County Sheriff's desert patrol, and federal authorities connected with the National Parks Service have lent their presence and authority to keeping the roughnecks away, or, if they came, under control at all times. This is one event which the legitimate rider can attend with the assurance that he will not have to leave because of any group of outlaws taking over.

Undoubtedly the greatest single factor in keeping the Run growing is the drawing power of Death Valley itself. There is hardly a man, woman or child in the western part of the U.S. who has not heard of it, and who has not vowed some day to see it. Steeped in legends of stranded wagon trains, lost gold and silver mines, and fabulous for its ghost towns and the part it played in the early development of borax it is enough to excite the imagination of the most sedentary individual and set him to yearning for the wide open spaces.

For that matter no other place in the West is set into spaces more wide open or inaccessible. From any angle it can be approached only after many miles of desert travel, and from all points it is entered only after traversing a substantial mountain range. The eastern approach is the highest where the Townes Pass entrance through the Panamint Range reaches 5,260 feet. Daylight Pass on the eastern entrance from Beatty is 4,317, the Summit Pass near Death Valley Junction is 3,042 and Salsberry Pass near Shoshone on the southeastern entrance is 3,325 feet.

The floor of Death Valley, part of the Pacific Ocean at one time, reaches 280 feet below sea level at Bad Water, and the elevation at Furnace Creek Ranch is minus 178 feet. Nearby the Devil's Golf Course stretches for miles with its sharp salt crystals defying any man or animal to attempt its crossing. Northward lie sand dunes, and even sections of fertile soil suitable for raising dates. Pure water is pumped from wells at Furnace Creek, as contrasted with poisonous lakes lying beneath some of the salt flats.

Mineral deposits in the mountain ranges surrounding Death Valley add pastel colors of pinks, greys, purples and yellows and their reflections in the slanting sun and shadows of early morning and evening are a never ending source of enjoyment and wonder to the viewer.

Death Valley was not always the tourist attraction of today. Up until about 30 years ago, roads into the area were hazardous to the extreme, and no one in his right mind and without plenty of spare tires, gasoline and water would attempt to reach it. It is thought that the bones of some excursioners are still bleaching at unknown spots in the blazing desert sun near Death Valley. And so the annual Death Valley Run grows larger year by year. How big will it become? How long will it last? No one knows for sure, but we can assume it will not grow smaller unless some unforseen calamity such as the outbreak of war or the outlawing of all motorcycle riding takes place, and neither one of these do we expect in the near future.

motorcycle photography

Susan Boswell demonstrates a Bell and Howell automatic camera. This is a nice little camera using 127 size film and a single shutter speed. Has a flash attachment.

CAMERAS AND PHOTOGRAPHY FOR MOTORCYCLISTS

by Cliff Boswell

Photography and motorcycling go hand in hand, so to speak. It is only necessary to observe a few motorcyclists at racing or touring events to conclude that most of them are camera fans as well as cycle fans. If the quality of photos and color slides brought home is good, the story they tell will be much better than words alone. A photograph does not forget.

Photographic equipment, of course, is available in a wide variety of makes and prices, from very simple to extremely complex. My advice to the person beginning a photography hobby, or who uses a camera but once or twice a year, is to buy a fairly inexpensive outfit with the least number of complicated settings or adjustments.

Built-in exposure meters are common, with many cameras having them connected directly to the lens opening and the shutter. With this combination all that is necessary is to point the camera and release the shutter. An electronic exposure meter of some kind, though, whether built-in or separate, is an indispensable item for any kind of color photography.

A large percentage of fuzzy pictures seen at slide shows is caused by a slight movement of the camera as the shutter is released, but this defect can be easily remedied by the use of a tripod. As most simple cameras employ a single shutter speed, about 1/35th second, it is almost impossible to hold them steadily enough to assure a sharp picture which will blow up to screen size or which

will make a good enlargement.

If a camera is to be hand held, a shutter speed of at least 1/60th second, preferably 1/125th, is required to stop all camera movement.

The basic pieces of equipment, then, for a shutter-bug are (1) camera, (2) exposure meter, (3) tripod. All items are available in a size easily carried in a shoulder bag or in panniers.

It is true that once in a while a very good picture will show up regardless of poor technique, but this is the exception rather than the rule. To produce consistently good results a few simple but basic steps must be followed. I will attempt to explain them here.

Simple cameras with no shutter speed settings are merely pointed at the subject, then the shutter is released. They must be steadied on some firm object—a tripod is best. If hand held, they should be gripped with both hands with the elbows pressed tightly against the body for steadiness, and the breath held while the shutter is being released. Complete directions for adjusting them according to sky condition, shade, etc., come with each roll of film and with the camera itself. If directions are followed carefully, good results can be obtained. Photographs made with these cameras are never as sharp as those taken through an expensive lens, but they can be very satisfactory.

Three separate settings are required on more complicated cameras, (1) focus, (2) adjust the shutter speed, (3) set the diaphragm opening— lens opening. All readings are taken directly from the exposure meter. Diaphragm or lens openings are designated as f-stops with f-22 usually indicating the smallest, and each succeeding number 16,

11, 8, 5.6, 4.5, 3.5, 2.8, etc., indicating an opening twice as large as the preceeding one. The smaller f-stops require slower shutter speeds than the larger ones. Action shots usually involve the use of a fast shutter speed and a large lens opening.

Some cameras are equipped with a system combining shutter speeds and f-stops in a manner that, once set, any change of shutter speed will automatically adjust the lens opening to compensate. This is called the EV system. Modern exposure meters include EV reading as well as shutter speeds and f-stops.

Exposure meters must always be set to the speed of the film being used before an accurate light reading can be taken. It is usually indicated as an ASA speed number.

Small f-stops, down to f-22, are used where great depth of field (distance between nearest and farthest objects in sharp focus) is desired. Most scenic shots require small f-stops. Close-ups or portraits where critical focusing upon a single object is desired may use larger f-stops and correspondingly faster shutter speeds.

Most modern cameras include a depth-of-field scale which indicates distance between objects in sharp focus at any particular lens setting or focusing point.

The normal lighting for daylight scenic shots is considered to be when the sun is above and slightly to the left of the photographer's position. An exposure meter will give a reliable reading from this position, but many sensational or unusual pictures are obtained in strong back light-

ing (when the camera is pointed almost directly into the sun), or in side lighting (when the sun is low on the horizon). Back lighted shots require at least double the exposure of normally lighted scenes, and here is where cameras with automatic light meter adjustments get into trouble—the meter will adjust for bright sunlight while everything being photographed is in heavy shadow.

A "rule of thumb," in this situation, is to point the meter away from the sun for a reading; then set the camera to one f-stop larger. If no adjustment is possible for an automatic camera, the photoelectric cell should be covered one-half while the exposure is being made. This will compensate for the additional exposure required.

All of these basic rules apply equally to motion picture as well as still cameras.

This has been a quick run-down on a highly complicated subject. If the amateur photographer will learn the basic concepts mentioned, and diligently study the instruction booklet furnished with his camera, he should derive a great deal of satisfaction from his prints and slides when they come back from the processor.

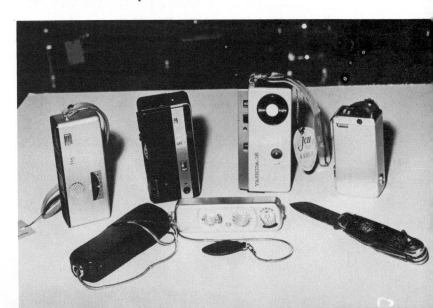

Deputy Chief H. W. Sullivan, Commander Traffic Bureau.

For controlling traffic and speeders the motorcycle officer certainly is the most effective. Many thousands of motorcycles are used by city, state, county and the government for traffic enforcement in certain areas. The largest user of motorcycles for police work is Los Angeles, California, with 556 Harley-Davidsons.

LOS ANGELES POLICE MOTOR SQUAD— LARGEST IN THE WORLD

Los Angeles was one of the first cities to inaugurate a squad of motorcycle policemen. Throughout the years, the motorcycle officer has been as much a part of the Los Angeles Police Department as the foot patrolman or the officers who drive in squad cars. Los Angeles has a larger area within its city limits to patrol than any other city in the world and today with 556 units has a larger number of Police motorcycles than any other department.

The Los Angeles motor officer is on duty the year around, night and day—and Los Angeles has, without a doubt, one of the most efficient motorcycle police departments in the world. We are indebted to the Traffic Education Section of the Los Angeles Police Department for furnishing us with the excellent photographs and the information contained in this story.

For the past thirty-four years, Harley-Davidsons have been used by the Los Angeles Police Department. Prior to that time, Indian, Henderson and Ace cycles had been used.

In addition to the large squad of 398 officers using solo motorcycles, the department also utilizes 110 Harley-Davidson three-wheelers for marking parked cars and controlling traffic in some sections. There are forty-eight more in a pool of extras. These three-wheelers are not included as a part of the motor squad, but they do increase the total number of motorcycles used and demonstrate the value of the three-wheeler for traffic control duty.

For traffic control there is no substitute for the uniformed motorcycle officer. His very presence, either in motion or standing anywhere, is a silent warning for the speeder or the reckless motorist to slow down or drive more carefully.

The Los Angeles Police Department's Traffic Bureau, commanded by Deputy Chief H. W. Sullivan, comprises four police divisions. One of these, the Traffic Enforcement Division, under the command of Captain Cliff Shannon, is generally referred to by those assigned to it as the "Motor Squad."

Begun in 1911 when six men were assigned to the original "Motorcycle Speed Squad," today's Traffic Enforcement Division is a modern unit of 350 men and motorcycles, covering the more than 459 square miles of city area. In 1964, the motor squad rolled 5,948,455 miles, or approximately 16,995 miles per officer.

Selection of men for the motor squad is stringent. An officer may volunteer after one year of service on the police department. The volunteer is then required to pass certain driver aptitude tests. Visual acuity, depth perception, reaction, coordination, and peripheral vision are of the

This is a group of 15 (a portion of 50) 1938 Indian Chiefs purchased by the California Highway Patrol. They were assigned for use by the Los Angeles C.H.P. office. Officer at left is Inspector Jerry Page, Los Angeles Indian Distributor. Clymer at right. Ed Kretz, Sr., then five year Clymer employee, assisted in assembling and delivering the machines.

Delivery of new 1920 Indian Chiefs for Los Angeles Police Department.

Los Angeles has always had one of the largest police squads in the U.S. and the first one which was organized in 1906. Shown here is a group of motor squad officers ready for inspection in 1924, on Indians.

Most familiar professional motorcycle rider is the traffic control policeman. Superb riders all, their training is extremely rigorous.

utmost importance to the officer who attempts to qualify for this potentially hazardous assignment. Next he will have to face the motor officer examining board. Here the officer must appear before three selected superior officers. His background, temperament, and special ability to meet the public are reviewed. The list of top qualifying officers is then presented to a command staff Motor Officer Selection Board. The few officers who qualify become the students of a Motor Officer Training Class.

The training program is under direct supervision of the department's Training Division. A strict curriculum is followed, the standard course being comprised of forty hours of classroom instruction and two weeks of riding instruction. Even experienced motorcycle riders may be "washed out" during the rigid field training, since maneuvering safely through city traffic demands exceptional riding skill.

Upon assignment to the squad the officer will ride a Harley-Davidson FLH 74 OHV Police Model. A complete knowledge of the nomenclature of this machine is the first step. This instruction is received by the student, both in the classroom and in the field training. At first, all riding is performed at low speeds, concentrating on balance and throttle and clutch control. Tight left and right turns must be practiced. Proper use of the foot and hand brake are taught. Each maneuver the motorcycle is capable of performing must be perfected by the rider during the term of his instruction. Although the motor officer's prime duty will be patrolling the surface streets,

many times he is called upon to respond to emergencies that may call for rough riding through canyons and over hills to the scene of a fire, an aircraft crash or other urgent call. The training necessarily includes all possible types of riding skill.

Classroom work entails advanced instruction in the California Vehicle Code and emphasizes the importance of adherence to the department's carefully developed techniques of officer-violator contact and selective enforcement principles.

Upon successful completion of his training, the officer is transferred to the Traffic Enforcement Division, where he will be assigned to ride his first three months, with a veteran motor officer as his partner.

It is said that a man can perform no better than the tools of his trade. Therefore, the 398 motorcycles assigned to the Traffic Enforcement Division must be kept in top mechanical condition. There must be spare motorcycles immediately available. The Los Angeles Police Department has a complete modern motorcycle shop for maintenance, repair and overhaul of its machines. This modern assembly-line type of shop can completely rebuild a motorcycle for less than one-half of the cost of a new motorcycle. A saving to the taxpayer and top equipment for the largest motor squad in the world is the result.

At present, the department has field-tested the new electric starting 74 FLH Police Model Harley-Davidson, and two are now in operation with more on order. All of the motorcycles are equipped with two-way radios.

The deployment plan for the Traffic Enforcement Division is based upon selective enforcement. Information for this plan is obtained by statistical study of traffic accident reports. Each motor officer is assigned a "beat." The "beats" are determined from statistical reviews of traffic accident occurrences for a given period of time on a particular street or section of street. Each traffic accident report is tabulated by time, location, and accident cause or violation. The "beat" assignment reflects adherence to the policy of selective enforcement. The assignment of the motor squad follows the accident frequency patterns.

The motor squad deployment includes the day, mid, and night watches, and the Special Problems Enforcement Section. This section controls enforcement on the city's freeways, conducts commercial vehicle enforcement, investigates reports of special traffic needs, and operates the police helicopter.

Freeway assignments cover complete patrol of all freeways within the city. Enforcement adheres to the same principles of selectivity.

The police helicopter furnishes the eyes for the freeway patrol. The observer in the helicopter reports traffic flow conditions by means of the police radio communications system, enabling the ground units to expedite freeway traffic movement.

The complaint squad is assigned to investigate special traffic problems. A citizen, complaining of a traffic problem which is not in a high frequency area, is interviewed, the problem is surveyed, and

enforcement is provided or traffic engineering solutions are recommended. Many times the statistical results of a radar check assist this squad in bringing about correction of a problem. However, radar is not used for actual law enforcement.

It is realized that traffic control motorcycle riding duty is hazardous at its best. A motor officer may be required to perform duties in locations not readily accessible to any other vehicle. Therefore, it is the purpose of the Los Angeles Police Department to provide the finest equipment and maintenance, and to present a realistic training program that will produce the most efficient and effective motor squad possible.—F.C.

The mounted police of the U.S. Army regulate traffic in many areas and military installations. (Below)

The typical police motorcycle is equipped with siren, red lights, two-way radios, windshields and safety bars. Shown here is the Louisville, Kentucky, Motorcycle Drill Team performing during a parade at the recent Indianapolis Festival Parade held the night before the Indianapolis 500-mile race. The Louisville Motor Corps and the Indianapolis Squad perform spectacular demonstrations of skillful riding. (Bottom)

West German policeman on BMW patrols frontier fence between East and West Germany, at Kaiserwinkel near Volkswagen in Wolfsburg. On Clymer's visit there the officer saw his first copy of CYCLE Magazine.

During her visit to Germany, Queen Elizabeth of England was escorted in all parades by German Motor Police mounted on BMW's. All over the world BMW's are used extensively by police departments. Some claim that in most countries, excepting the U.S. and England, more BMW's are used for police duty than any other make.

Motorcycles are used to speed up deliveries by many business firms, including this TV-News messenger shown here.

Fun on or off the campus. Thousands of students across the nation are now using motorcycles and scooters for transportation to and from their classes. It is the most economical transportation to be had. (Below)

This specialized machine is built to carry the intrepid hunter or explorer. Strictly for mud, sand, rocks, it even floats!

motorcycles have many uses

CYCLE Editors, Abrams and Frazer, try out new bikes in various tests.

Madison Avenue's newest symbol of youth, freshness, clean-as-all-outdoors—the young motorcycling couple. (Left)

Lightweights (under 100cc) have simplified parking, made commuting a pleasure at campuses, office buildings and industrial plants across the nation. (Below)

Motorcycles take up far less parking space than automobiles. Many grade, high school and college parking lots are now partially filled with motorcycles and some parking lots have special space allotted for motorcycles and scooters.

Riders planning a charity drive for Muscular Dystrophy. (Right)

Many motion picture and TV companies use three-wheel motorcycles like this Harley-Davidson to transport cameramen and equipment. (Center)

Tom Welfley with red spot flashing passes under Cape direction sign with a load of film. (Below)

The rental of motorcycles is now a big business and there are rental facilities available in nearly all vacation spots throughout the U.S. Shown here is a group of Yamahas being transported on a special trailer which makes it possible to move the machines from one vacation spot to another. In other words, the rental operator follows the vacationists wherever they go. For cycle-less friends (or trailer-less owners) one solution is to have a party, rent machines for all! (Bottom)

162

Gil Stratton, noted TV and radio sportswriter and commentator, is often seen astride his Triumph twin on his way to cover events. (Far left)

Famous race-car driver Dan Gurney finds motorcycling a new challenge; he's ridden in many competitive cycle events including famous Big Bear contest. (Left)

Star Janet Leigh and broker-husband Bob Brandt emphasize togetherness. Bob sometimes competes in dirt track events. (Below, left)

Popular singer Dean Martin is relatively new to motorcycling but one of its strongest supporters.

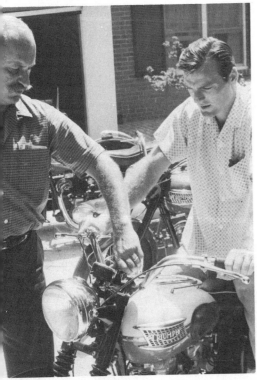

Actor Keenan Wynn (a motorcyclist from way back) is noted for his skill; a new enthusiast is Olympic Decathlon Champion, Bob Mathias.

Popular screen and TV star, Steve McQueen, is an enthusiastic motorcyclist and competed in the recent International Six Days Trials.

Stars, Ann-Margret and Jesse Pearson, used big Norton in movie, "Bye-Bye Birdie"; Ann now rides lightweight machine for fun. 163

Veteran West Coast road racing
star, John McLaughlin, and his fast
Norton.

Carroll Resweber was for several
years the number one motorcycle
racing champion in the U.S.

164

Some years ago, Ed Kretz was a top competition star. He went into the motorcycle business without previous business experience. Ed and his son Eddie have been extremely successful, and operate one of the most attractive motorcycle stores in the United States. There are many other fine motorcycle establishments —many of them operated by former competition men. (Far left)

Walter K. von Schonfeld, the "spark-plug" who sponsors motorcycle road racing events in U.S. under A.A.M.R.R. sanction and F.I.M. rules. (Left)

Al Bondy (center), U.S. importer of German BMW motorcycles, is shown with BMW officials at the assembly line of the factory in Munich, Germany. (Top)

When the Boston Braves moved to Milwaukee, Warren Spahn then a Milwaukee Brave, was a popular pitcher, as he still is today. Shown here is Spahn in the sidecar of a "Topper" scooter with Walter Davidson as the driver. (Bottom)

It is estimated that there were over 100 different makes of motorcycles manufactured in the United States since the inception of the industry. We list below 91 makes.

In some instances only a few machines were made. Unlike the automobile industry, few records of motorcycle production figures are available. We believe this is correct information—although we are sure that there were other makes manufactured on which no records are available.

A.C.E.	A.C.E. Motor Corporation, Philadelphia, Pa.	1919-1929
A.M.C.	Allied Motor Corporation, Chicago, Ill.	1912-1915
American	American Motorcycle Corp., Chicago, Ill.	1911-1914
Apache	Brown & Beck, Denver, Colo.	1907-1911
Auto-Bi	Buffalo Automobile Co., Buffalo, N.Y.	1902-1912
Autoped	Autoped Co. of America, New York	1915-1921
Arrow	Arrow Motor Co., Chicago, Ill.	-1914
Badger		1920-1921
Bayley-Flyer	Bayley-Flyer Autocycle Co., Chicago, Ill.	1913-1917
	McLeod-Manufacturing Co., Portland, Oreg.	1913-1917
Champion	Champion Motorcycle Mfg. Co., St. Louis, Mo.	1911-1913
Cleveland	Cleveland Motorcycle Co., Cleveland, Ohio	1915-1929
Columbia	Columbia Company, Westfield, Mass.	1900-1905
Crocker	Crocker Motorcycle Co., Los Angeles, Calif.	1934-1941
Cushman	Cushman Motors, Lincoln, Nebr.	1941-
Curtiss	Glenn Curtiss Mfg. Co., Hammondsport, N.Y.	1902-1910
Cycle-Scoot	Cycle-Scoot Co., Rockford, Ill.	1953-1955
Cyclone	Joerns Motor Mfg Co., St. Paul, Minn.	1913-1920
Dayton	Huffmann Mfg. Co., Elkhard, Ind.	1911-1917
DeLuxe	Excelsior Cycle Co., Chicago, Ill.	1912-1915
Duck	Duck Motorcycle Co., Stockton, Calif.	1906-1908
Dyke	Dyke Cycles, St. Louis, Mo.	1903-1906
Evans	Cyclemotor Corporation, Rochester, N.Y.	1919-1924
Excelsior	Excelsior Supply Co., Chicago, Ill.	1908-1911
	Excelsior Motor Mfg. & Supply Co., Chicago, Ill.	1911-1931
Emblem	Emblem Mfg. Co., Angola, N.Y.	1909-1925
Eagle	Eagle Motor Works, Minneapolis, Minn.	
Erie	Motorcycle Equip. & Supply Co., Hammondsport, N.Y.	1905-1915
Fairchild	Fairchild Motorcycle Co., Pasadena, Calif.	
Feilbach-Limited	Feilback Motor Co. Ltd., Milwaukee, Wis.	1912-1915
Flanders	Flanders Mfg. Co., Pontiac, Mich.	1911-1914
Flying Merkel	Miami Cycle & Mfg. Co., Middletown, Ohio (First ones were built by Joe Merkel in Milwaukee, Wis.)	1909-1915
Freyer & Miller	Freyer & Miller Mfg. Co., Cleveland, Ohio	1902-1905
Geer	Harry R. Geer Co., St. Louis, Mo.	1905-1909
Greyhound	Thomas-Greyhound Co., Buffalo, N.Y.	1907-1914
Harley-Davidson	Harley-Davidson Motor Co., Milwaukee, Wis.	1903 to date
Henderson	Henderson Motor Co., Detroit, Mich.	1911-1912
	Excelsior Motor Mfg. & Supply Co., Chicago, Ill.	1918-1931
Hilaman	A. L. Hilaman Co., Moorestown, N.J.	1906-1915
Holley	Holley Motor Co., Bradford, Pa.	1902-1910

Imperial		1903-1910
Indian	Hendee Manufacturing Co., Springfield, Mass.	
	Indian Motorcycle Co., Springfield, Mass. ..	1901-1953
Iver-Johnson	Iver Johnson's Arts & Cycle Works, Fitchburg, Mass.	1907-1915
Jefferson	Waverley Mfg. Co., Jefferson, Wis.	1911-1914
Kenzler-Waverley	Kenzler-Waverley Motorcycle Co., Cambridge, Mass.	1910-1914
Marathon		1910
Marsh	Marsh Motorcycle Mfg. Co., Brockton, Mass.	1901-1920
Marvel	Marvel Motorcycle Co., Hammondsport, N.Y.	1910-1913
Merkel	Merkel Manufacturing Co., Milwaukee, Wis.	1902-1922
Miami	Miami Cycle & Mfg. Co., Middletown, Ohio	1905-1923
Michaelson	Michaelson Motor Co., Minneapolis, Minn.	1910-1915
Militaire	Militaire Auto Co., Inc., Cleveland, Ohio	
	Militaire Mfg. Co., Buffalo, N.Y.	1911-1920
Minneapolis	Minneapolis Motorcycle Co., Minneapolis, Minn.	1901-1915
Mitchell	Wisconsin Wheel Works, Racine, Wis.	1901-1910
M.M.	American Motor Co., Brockton, Mass.	1906-1915
Monarch	Ives Motorcycle Corp., Oswego, N.Y.	1912-1915
Montgomery-Ward	Montgomery-Ward, Chicago, Ill.	1911-1912
Mustang	Mustang Motorcycle Corp., Glendale, Calif.	1946 to date
Neracar	Neracar Corporation, Syracuse, N.Y.	1921-1926
New Era	New Era Autocycle Co., Dayton, Ohio	1906-1913
N.S.U.	N.S.U. Motor Co., New York, N.Y.	
Orient	Waltham Mfg., Co., Waltham, Mass.	1900-1910
Peerless	Peerless Motorcycle Co., Boston, Mass.	1913-1916
P.E.M.	Perry E. Mack, Jefferson, Wis.	
Pierce	Pierce Motorcycle Co., Buffalo, N.Y.	1909-1913
Pirate	Milwaukee Motorcycle Co., Milwaukee, Wis.	1913-1915
Pope	Pope Mfg. Co., Hartford, Conn.	1908-1916
Powell	Powell Mfg. Co., Compton, Calif.	1944-1946
Rambler	Jefferey & Gormeley, Racine, Wis.	1903-1915
Reading-Standard	Reading-Standard Co., Reading, Pa.	1903-1922
Reliance	Reliance Motorcycle Co., Oswego, N.Y.	1912-1915
Schickel	Schickel Motor Co., Stamford, Conn.	1912-1915
Sears	Sears, Roebuck & Co., Chicago, Ill.	1912-1916
Shaw	Shaw Mfg. Co., Galesburg, Kans.	1907-1912
Simplex	Simplex Mfg. Corp., New Orleans, La.	1936-
Spacke	Spacke Co., Indianapolis, Ind.	1911-1914
Steffey	Steffey Motorcycle & Mfg. Co., Philadelphia, Pa.	1902-1905
Super X	Excelsior Motor Mfg. & Supply Co., Chicago, Ill.	1924-1931
Thiem	Joerns-Thiem Motor Co., St. Paul, Minn. ..	1903-1914
Thor	Aurora Automatic Machinery Co., Aurora, Ill.	1903-1916
Tiger	Tiger Autobike Co., Chicago, Ill.	1915-1916
Tribune		1903-1915
Vard	Vard Mfg. Co., Pasadena, Calif.	1954-
Triumph	Triumph Mfg. Co., Detroit City, Mich.	1912-
Wagner	Wagner Motorcycle Co., St. Paul, Minn.	1901-1914
Waverley	Waverley Mfg. Co., Jefferson, Wis.	
Westover	Westover Co., Denver, Colo.	1912-1913
Whizzer	Whizzer International, Inc., Pontiac, Mich.	1947-1954
Williams	J. Newton Williams, New York, N.Y.	1917-
Woods	J. J. Woods Co., Denver, Colo.	1911-1912
Yale	Consolidated Mfg. Co., Toledo, Ohio	1902-1915
Yankee		1922-1923

yesterday

This unique steam motorcycle was built by a Mr. Copeland in 1885, during the heyday of high-wheel bicycles. Note the inverted steam engine mounted below the handlebars and the boiler above the front wheel.

This section includes photos, articles and reproductions of advertising pertaining to early makes of motor vehicles.

The history of the motorcycle industry in this country is fascinating. As we look back over the years it seems that the motorcycles that once appeared to be so well designed and engineered are really crude and unfinished when compared to the beautifully designed and engineered bikes that are available to riders today.

The engineers, the competition riders and the manufacturers that have long since passed out of the motorcycle picture also deserve much credit for their efforts and the obstacles that they had to overcome in building a motorcycle market in a country where automobiles have a much greater hold on the public than motorcycles. It would greatly please many of the pioneers of this industry if they could see today the present popularity of motorcycling and the new image that has been brought about by the efforts of thousands of fine manufacturers, importers, dealers and riders.

The world's first motor bicycle was built in Germany by Gottlieb Daimler in 1885. It had a vertical engine with belt drive to rear wheel. It is now displayed in the Daimler-Benz Museum at Unterturkheim (suburb of Stuttgart). The Daimler Company now makes Mercedes-Benz cars.

171

Could this have been the first one-horsepower bike? (It was built in England in 1829.)

Early British motorcycles. In the early days, England and other foreign countries produced some unique motorcycles, as evidenced by these photographs. A well-known type of one-cylinder motor tricycle, the Leon Bollee, which came out in 1896. (Center)

Probably the first tricar. A machine built by Humbers in 1898, and called the "Olympic Tandem." This was one of Pennington's designs. (Bottom)

Wonder what today's S.P.C.A. would have to say—and the newspapers? Some journals of the 1870's seriously commented on the Cynophere advertisement, while one suggested that "no respectable canine need take hydrophobia—a new and far more honorable field of operations is open to him if he will but improve the golden opportunity offered by the Cynophere."

1875

THE CYNOPHERE.

Invented by M. Huret, of Paris, France, and Patented in the United States, December 14, 1875.

The Cynophere consists of two large wheels, between which is a comfortable seat and rest for the feet. In front is a small guide wheel, the direction being controlled at will by a rod held in the right hand, while at the left is a brake by which the speed is regulated. Power is furnished by a dog within each of the side wheels, and so light is the draft that it is no more exertion for the dogs to run upon the treadway of the wheel than it is for them to go at the same speed at their own pleasure. The French Society for the Prevention of Cruelty to Animals, to whom the subject was submitted by the inventor, unanimously endorsed the system.

The vehicle is light and graceful in its mechanism, and can be used by ladies and children, as well as gentlemen, without the slightest danger, discomfort or exertion. For pleasure purposes it is unsurpassed, and when fully introduced to the American public is destined to achieve a popularity far greater than that of the velocipede, while the moderate expense will bring it within the easy reach of all.

Michaux's steam bicycle (1867)

DAIMLER 1885

MILLET 1892

BUTLER 1889

GLADIATOR 1895

DE DION 1895

H & W 1893

Butler's tricycle had two cylinders driving direct; the H. & W. also had direct drive. The Millet employed the rotative engine.

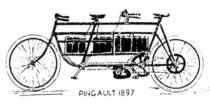

PINGAULT 1897

Early electric vehicles: all employed chain drive, obtaining the necessary reduction by the use of a large driven sprocket

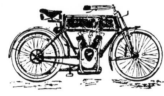

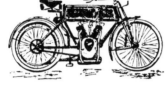

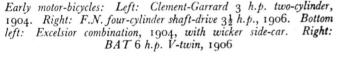

Early motor-bicycles: Left: Clement-Garrard 3 h.p. two-cylinder, 1904. Right: F.N. four-cylinder shaft-drive 3½ h.p., 1906. Bottom left: Excelsior combination, 1904, with wicker side-car. Right: BAT 6 h.p. V-twin, 1906

Left: Quadrant twin-engined tri-car, 1904, with two 2½ h.p. engines, one driving by chain, and one by belt. Right: Atlas de Dion quadricycle, 1904

Top, left: Eureka 3½ h.p. front-drive quad, 1901. Right: Singer 2½ h.p. 2-seater tricycle, 1902, with the engine inside the front wheel Bottom, left: Aurora motor-cycle. Right: Humber 2 h.p. motor-cycle, 1902, with primary and secondary chain drive

Some motor-bicycles of 1900: Top, left: Werner front-wheel drive. Right: Holden, direct-driven, with pedal-operated crypto gear on front wheel. Bottom, left: Centaure. Right: Aster-engined Orient

Diagrams showing how unsettled were manufacturers' ideas as to the best place to put the engine: 1900-1901. (Right)

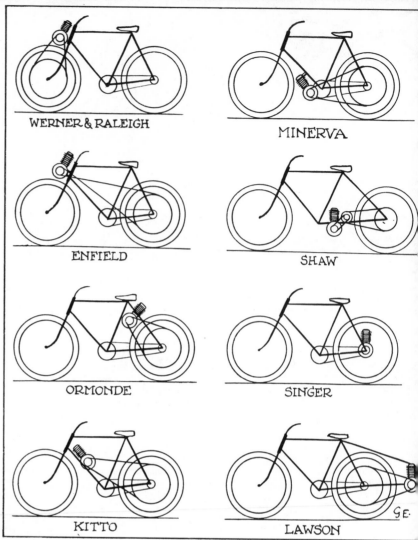

WERNER & RALEIGH

MINERVA

ENFIELD

SHAW

ORMONDE

SINGER

KITTO

LAWSON

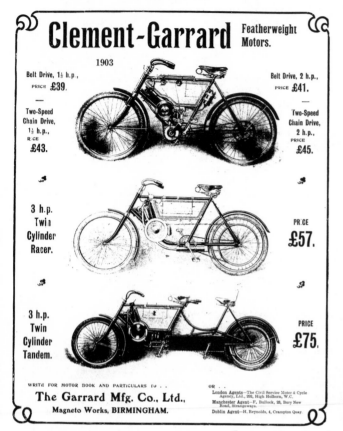
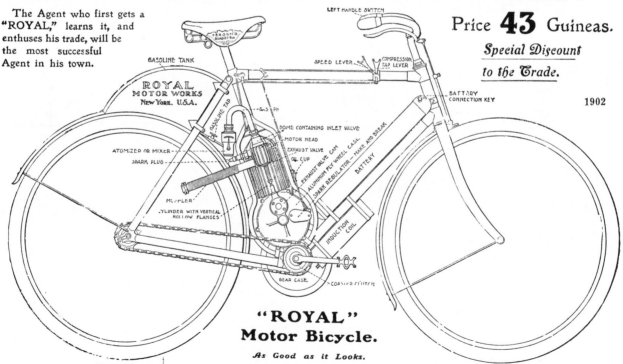

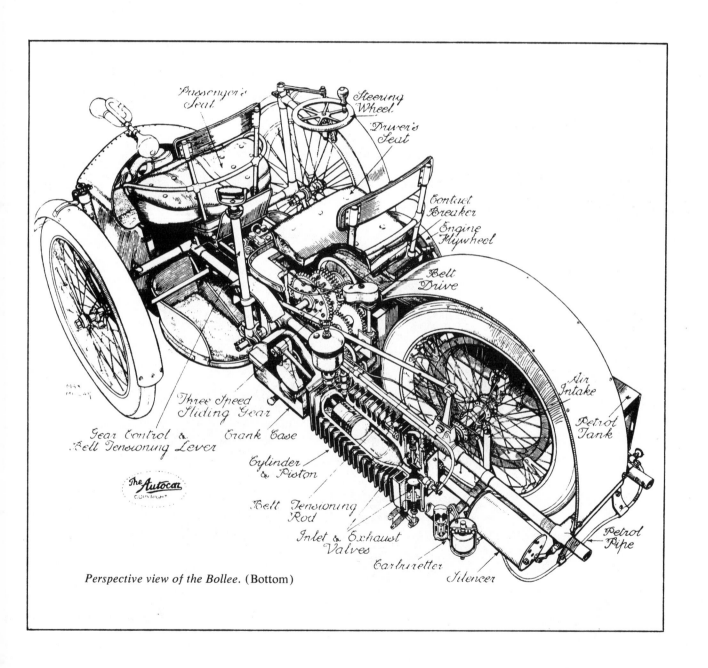

Passenger's Seat

Steering Wheel

Driver's Seat

Contact Breaker

Engine Flywheel

Belt Drive

Air Intake

Petrol Tank

Three Speed Sliding Gear

Gear Control & Belt Tensioning Lever

Crank Case

The Autocar COPYRIGHT

Cylinder & Piston

Belt Tensioning Rod

Inlet & Exhaust Valves

Carburetter

Silencer

Petrol Pipe

Perspective view of the Bollee. (Bottom)

The Royal Enfield motor bicycle of 1901 which claimed to have some advantages over the Raleigh and Werner. (Right)

Coventry Eagle motor bicycle fitted with an M.M.C. engine and shown towing a trailer. (Below)

The Copeland Steam Motorcycle was built in Los Angeles in 1884 by the Copeland Brothers. The machine would do about eight miles an hour for short distances. (Below right)

A tandem motor bicycle driven by an electric motor and accumulators. Built by Humbers in 1898.

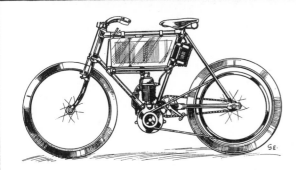

The new type Werner which altered the design of motorcycles.

An unusual Norton two-stroke utility lightweight.

Singer's motor wheel fitted to a tricycle.

A Beeston two-seater motorcycle of 1898, typical of the motorcycle "combination" of that period.

Even before the turn of the century, manufacturer Pennington of England had the Madison Avenue touch in advertising his products. Here the Pennington, with the engine in the rear, is shown high in the air jumping a canal, while horrified spectators look on.

by EMMETT MOORE

The wiry young man on the little red motor bicycle was obviously nervous. Beads of perspiration stood on his brow as he wiped his hands on his trouser legs and firmly grasped the stubby handlebars. Again, he eyed the steep, cobblestoned street ahead and the little group of men atop the grade perhaps a quarter mile away. Curious onlookers stopped to gape for a motor bicycle was a rare thing to see on a sunny morning in May of 1901. It was spring in Springfield, Massachusetts, and a memorable day in American motorcycle history — the first prototype Indian was about to be tested.

The somewhat moist young man was Carl Oscar Hedstrom and the motor bicycle was his own handiwork. Much depended on the happenings of the next few moments. The young engineer bent to make a final adjustment of his carburetor, then as one of the more portly of the men atop the hill waved a handkerchief, he twirled the pedals and the little single broke into lusty life.

Fifty-three years later the events of that afternoon remain bright in the memory of this same man who so convincingly sailed up Cross Street hill long ago. Oscar Hedstrom retired to his estate near the little town of Portland, Connecticut. Despite his eighty-three summers, he was still fairly spry and active, able to relish a discussion of the many interesting events in the years of his connection with the motorcycle industry until his death.

Before Hedstrom died, this writer fulfilled an

First Indian twin made its appear-
ance in 1905. The rear cylinder formed
part of the frame. The company claimed
a hundred thousand of them in use (Top)

The Indian "Powerplus" motor,
brought out in 1916, featured side
by side valves for the first time. This
model was used with great success
by American dispatch riders in
World War I.

ambition of some years standing — to meet and to talk to this grand old pioneer motorcycle designer — the father of a breed of bikes which have a special place in the heart of many an American. At the time of our meeting, Hedstrom was one of the very few living men who were working with motorcycles before 1900. Introductions were made by my companion on the short ride from Springfield, traditional home of Indian. This was none other than Erle "Pop" Armstrong — he of the once red thatch, the motordromes and the board tracks.

Seated in the comfortable Hedstrom living room, with its trophies and its ultramodern TV set, the figures of long ago motorcycle men and forgotten machines once more came to life. Here we literally hung on the words of this unique figure who had lived through the entire span of motorcycle history.

Hedstrom's story begins in the little town of Smolen, Sweden, where he was born March 12, 1871. When he was only nine, his parents emigrated and settled in Brooklyn, N.Y. Here, in a pre-baseball Brooklyn (imagine!), the big sport of the day was bicycling. Everyone — man, woman, and child rode a bike. Oscar was no exception: as soon as he was old enough he persuaded his father to buy him one of the expensive wheels. He remembers this bike — "a Victor — with a real spring fork!" As he grew into young manhood, he became more proficient in the art of pedal pushing and developed a talent for dusting off his rivals in the "scorching" sessions. This penchant for speed led to his entering professional bicycle racing, and here, too, he

proved to be a top-notch performer.

Some time after his entry into bicycle racing, the first motor pacing tandems began to make

their appearance. This speedier type of machine caught Hedstrom's fancy and he transferred his activities to the motorized jobs. His partner in this somewhat risky enterprise was one George Henshaw, and for some time the team of "Hedstrom and Henshaw" was unbeatable — as long as their machine ran. The fact that the huge clumsy pacing tandems were unreliable and hard to manage led to delays and dangerous spills. This situation bore looking into, and Oscar was just the lad for the job.

It didn't take the young cyclist long to find out that if he wanted a better bike there was only one way to get it — build it himself. Although this was a truly formidable project in those dark days of internal combustion design, he tackled the job. The frame was built up in his own workshop and a specially "tuned" De Dion engine was incorporated. This machine proved a success from the start, and soon had him busy making duplicates to order.

Among the spectators watching the races was one who had more than a casual interest. The speed of the Hedstrom tandem caught the eye of this man — one George Hendee, bicycle manufacturer from Springfield, Massachusetts. And thereby, friend, hangs quite a tale!

Hendee, a former bicycle champion in his own right, had quite a good sized bicycle plant at Springfield. For some time he had been toying with the idea of producing a motor bicycle, and the Hedstrom machine's performance brought his train of thought to a conclusion. He approached Oscar with the proposition to design a light ma-

chine suitable for everyday road use — transportation for the millions was his idea in those dim pre-Model T days. This idea was right in line with Hedstrom's own, so a deal was made on the spot. A contract was written on the back of an old envelope, and signed by both men.

The young inventor immediately retired to his home at Middletown, Connecticut, and set to work making drawings for the new machine. Castings were made at a local foundry and machined in his own workshop. So speedily did he work, that inside of three months the first machine had been transferred from an idea into a complete motor bicycle. After the test as described in the opening paragraphs of this tale, the "Indian" motorcycle was placed in production and demand soon exceeded capacity to supply.

Something had to be done to speed production, and Hedstrom began to seek an outside supplier which could manufacture motors to his exacting specification. He finally located such a firm in far off Aurora, Illinois. This was the Aurora Automatic Machine Co., later to become known as the manufacturers of the famous "Thor" motorcycles. (The name lives today — unglamourously, but with a large selling in electrical appliances and such!) A deal was soon made with the Illinois firm to supply motors. This arrangement involved the Aurora plant using Hedstrom-designed motors in their own motorcycles. "But we always did a little something to the motors we received from them" chuckles Hedstrom, "Couldn't have Thors passing our Indians on the road you know!"

180

Thor was an early producer of motorcycles and engines in the U.S. The first Indians and many other early makes used Thor engines. Shown here is a 2-3/4 h.p. Thor of 1902. (Left and below)

"What happened to the first Indian?" repeated the old gentleman in answer to my query at this point. "Well, the very first machine does not exist. I broke it up and used some of the parts in later machines."

The year 1906 rolled around — Hendee production was growing by leaps and bounds, and the future looked rosy indeed. Rival factories were springing up all over the country, and Hedstrom decided that the Indian needed some additional publicity. The opportunity for this presented itself when speed trials were announced to be held at Ormond Beach, Florida — just south of the present road beach course.

A special machine was carefully prepared, and upon arrival at Ormond, Hedstrom found himself pitted against such titans of the day as Alexander Winton with his "Bullet," a brace of rakish looking Oldsmobile "Torpedos" and other four-wheeled speed creations.

The 1906 Indian held up its name with honor. During the trials, the machine with Hedstrom himself riding turned the 5 miles distance in 5.27 — second only to the huge, flame-belching "Bullet" itself. In a handicap race, the motorcycle came in second on time, "but Winton never did actually pass me!" says Oscar with satisfaction almost a half-century later!

Perhaps the most amusing episode recounted by our host concerned a race meet held at a cer-

THE THOR MOTOR BICYCLE

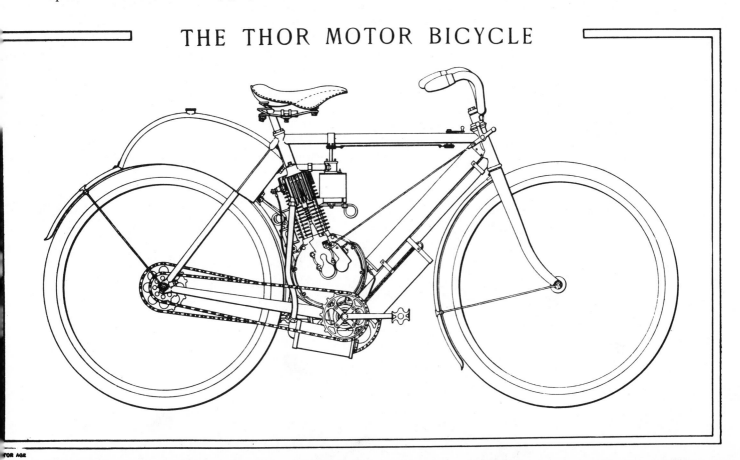

tain fashionable horse racing circuit not far from Springfield. "This was billed as a gentleman's race," smiled Hedstrom, "so naturally I assumed that I would be eligible to ride." Arriving upon the scene of action with his "redskin" the young designer-rider was quietly, but firmly, given the well-known brush off. He was told that the program was filled and that there was no room for additional entries. Oscar smelled a rat. His suspicions were confirmed when the field lined up for the start — all mounted on Pope motorcycles, product of a rival manufacturer! This was a set-up if ever there was one!

Biding his time, he waited until the event was run, then requested permission to ride an exhibition mile. This was reluctantly granted — and to quote the old-timer "Boy, I made those gentlemen's times look sick!"

For some years after this, Hedstrom continued to take personal part in races, runs and endurance contests. Many of the early manufacturers did this, including the founders of the Harley-Davidson factory who were endurance grind specialists. The old-timers were quite willing to go to any length to demonstrate the quality of their product.

Perhaps the pinnacle of Hedstrom's success came when he accompanied a quartet of the red machines to the Isle of Man in 1911. Here he was privileged to witness a feat that has seldom been repeated — three riders of the same team finished as one — two — three. Riders were O. C. Godfrey, on the winner, C. B. Franklin second, and A. J. Moorhouse third. That was a great day in Indian history! Franklin later took Hedstrom's place as chief engineer at Indian.

In 1913, at the age of forty-two, Hedstrom had achieved financial independence. His relations with his partner were somewhat strained at this time, so he decided that this would be a good time to quit. He resigned his position with the Hendee Manufacturing Co. and retired.

At the time of his retirement, the Hendee Manufacturing Co. — as Indian was then known — had grown to a giant enterprise. The main factory occupied a building of wedge-shape over three city blocks long and five stories high. Besides this, there was a large addition in East Springfield known as "Hendeeville." Production at one time approached 400 motorcycles per day.

In 1917, Hedstrom returned to the Indian factory to help perfect the machines then in production. This time he stayed for over a year. During this period and all through World War I, he served on the Advisory Board of the Army Quartermaster Corps.

Following his second retirement, he again returned to his estate at Portland and began the years long work of developing and improving his land. In his more active years he was an enthusiastic sportsman and found enjoyment in game-bird and duck shooting. At one time he raced power boats, and was Connecticut State Champion with his "Indian."

He is now deceased. The Indian name is now gone as well. After building bikes for a few years with the Indian name in England, production ended in the early sixties.

harley-davidson —
a pioneer and
still going strong

The Davidsons and Bill Harley.
These men were the ones who
founded the Harley-Davidson Com-
pany. From left to right—Chief
Engineer William S. Harley, Shop
Superintendent William Davidson
(father of the present President,
William Davidson). Seated is the first
President Walter Davidson, and at
right is Sales Manager Arthur
Davidson. All are deceased.

Shown here are current officials of the Harley-Davidson Motor Company. From left to right, Gordon Davidson, Walter Davidson, William Harley and President, William Davidson. All are sons of the original Harley-Davidson owners. (Opposite left)

Attractive back-seat riders of 1913 were not bashful in boosting their favorite make. At left can be seen a tandem seat which was popular for the passenger. (Below)

One early model of each Harley-Davidson is on display in this room at the factory at Milwaukee starting with the first Harley-Davidson of 1904. (Opposite, bottom)

IGNAZ SCHWINN

by FLOYD CLYMER

This pen drawing of Ignaz Schwinn was made about 1911 when he acquired the Excelsior Supply Company in Chicago. Mr. Schwinn, a German immigrant, brazed bicycle frames for $3.50 a day. He soon formed his own company, Arnold-Schwinn and Company, and they started manufacturing mail-order bicycles for Montgomery Ward, Butler Brothers and others. The bicycle business continued to grow and so did the sale of Excelsior motorcycles. In 1918 Mr. Schwinn and his son, Frank, purchased the assets of the defunct Henderson Motorcycle Company of Detroit. From that time until 1931 the Excelsior Motor Manufacturing and Supply Company manufactured both Excelsior and 4-cylinder Henderson motorcycles.

As a Schwinn distributor in Colorado, Wyoming and New Mexico for many years, I had a close business association with Mr. Schwinn, his son

Frank and his associates. He was a fine man and known as "the little giant" in the motorcycle business. He was stubborn, opinionated, a hard worker with a sense of responsibility and one who had no time for shirkers.

He became one of the wealthiest men in Chicago through his efforts, and today the bicycle firm which he founded is operated by his grandsons and is the largest bicycle factory in America — the name Schwinn on a bicycle is like Tiffany on jewelry.

During my business association with many individuals and firms, I have never had a kinder feeling for anyone than I had for Mr. Schwinn. He helped me through my early days in the motorcycle business by extending liberal credit, he supplied me with many racing machines and cooperated in advertising programs. He was a rugged individualist and a one-man operator. Although his son, Frank, had much influence in later years over Mr. Schwinn's operations, during the years I knew him he came to the motorcycle factory every day and made a regular tour of the plant. After his morning inspection at the motorcycle plant he would usually go to the bicycle factory on North Kildare Street where he enjoyed sitting beside his old fashioned roll-top desk and personally directing the operations of the bicycle factory. The success of Ignaz Schwinn is ample proof that there are great possibilities for a poor immigrant to build a successful business in this country, even though he started with the handicaps of a language barrier and very little money.

When I was seven years old, I learned to drive a curved-dash Oldsmobile purchased by my father, Dr. J. B. Clymer, who was a physician and surgeon in the small town of Berthoud at the foot of the Rocky Mountains, 50 miles north of Denver, Colorado.

When I was eleven, I was a dealer for Reo, Maxwell and Cadillac and sold 26 in two years.

The first motorcycle I owned was a Yale-California, which I owned only a few weeks. I kept needling my Dad for another motorcycle, and he suggested I get the agency for some make. I could not get Indian, but a series of high pressure letters and attractive catalogues sold me on the Thomas-Bi, built in Buffalo, New York.

In 1912 I rode and won my first amateur race on a ½-mile track in Boulder, Colorado. Later, I rode a Merkel and an Indian on dirt tracks in the Rocky Mountain States.

In 1914, I moved to Greeley, Colorado and opened a motorcycle store, handling Excelsior. Later on, I added Harley-Davidson to my line.

I raced for many years, and won the first professional hillclimb up 14,105-foot Pike's Peak.

Later, I rode on the Harley-Davidson team at Dodge City, Kansas, where I broke the World's Hour Record for dirt tracks, covering 84 miles the first hour, and averaged 83 miles an hour for the first 100 miles.

I also rode with a partner, Frank Kunce, in the enactment of the Pony Express Relay; however, we used motorcycles instead of ponies. A number of messengers on motorcycles stationed in different cities from Washington, D.C. to San Francisco carried a pouch containing a message from President Woodrow Wilson to the President of the Pan-Pacific Exposition in San Francisco for the opening of the Exposition.

Later I moved from Greeley to Denver, where I became Indian, Excelsior and Henderson distributor for the states of Colorado, Wyoming and New Mexico.

After disposing of the motorcycle business, I manufactured automobile accessories, including the Clymer windshield spotlight, mounted through the car windshield glass.

During the time I was in the motorcycle business, I raced on dirt tracks and made many cross-country records on motorcycles and in automobiles.

I competed in many hillclimbs, and three times won the then-famous Capistrano Hillclimb in Orange County, California.

After disposing of my automobile accessories business, I took the Harley-Davidson agency in Denver, and also had a branch Harley-Davidson agency in Kansas City, Missouri, later selling this interest to Perry E. Davis.

I then moved to Los Angeles, where I first handled foreign makes, and later became the Los Angeles Indian distributor.

In 1944, I started publishing books on automotive subjects, including motorcycles. In 1953, I purchased *Cycle* magazine from Bob Petersen, who was then, and who still is, publisher of *Motor Trend*.

With the acquisition of *Cycle*, I was again part

of the motorcycle fraternity in which I had spent many of the happiest years of my life. *Cycle* circulation has increased from 30,000 to 113,000 a month in 12 years.

As one who has been connected with the motorcycle business in some capacity for so many years, I am extremely happy over the motorcycle boom, and the tremendous increase in motorcycling popularity. Thus, when McGraw-Hill requested that I do a book for them on motorcycles (I had already written four for them on automobiles) I jumped at the chance.

This book is not intended to be a complete history of the motorcycle industry, for to compile such a book would require tremendous additional research, and would, no doubt, require ten volumes to complete.

There are many motorcycles not illustrated or mentioned in this book, some because we did not receive requested information, and in other instances the facts were unobtainable.

I do believe, however, that this, the most complete book ever compiled on modern and historical motorcycles, will prove interesting to the reader. I hope so. — Floyd Clymer.

I looked
like this
in 1907

...and this is the ad that got me ➡

I was SOLD on the Auto-Bi even before I went to Denver and bought my demonstrator. Consider the appeal of this ad. . . . I wanted to be up-to-date and the ad "admitted" Auto-Bi had THE motorcycle for 1907. . . . I wanted POWER, as I lived at the foot of the Rocky Mountains . . . I wanted SPEED to beat the other fellow . . . and I wanted SIMPLICITY and COMFORT . . . and the ad stated AUTO-BI had all these features . . . and they wanted LIVE agents (that sounded flattering) . . . and the cylinder inclined so that the air would blow on the head while in motion to cool it better (so the sales manager told me later). I had already written for the catalogue and found out the "TERMS" mentioned were CASH.

The illustration here shows the "cheaper" model. I bought the better De Luxe model! .

Now I ask you . . . IF you had been 12 years old and wanted a motorcycle agency . . . wouldn't this ad have appealed to you, too?

—*Clymer.*

NEXT TO FLYING

Model
No. 45

Price,
$175

IMMEDIATE DELIVERY

MR. DEALER:

To be up-to-date you need the 1907 Thomas Auto-Bi Agency. We have THE motorcycle for 1907.

The MOST POWERFUL and speedy single cylinder machine on the market.

The SIMPLEST motorcycle ever built.

POWER

Of course you want to climb hills and negotiate rough ROADS EASILY AND COMFORTABLY. The 3 H.P of the No. 45 Thomas Auto-Bi is REAL POWER.

Every part of this machine is built for the exact purpose for which it is used. It s not a miscellaneous collection of parts placed on a bicycle.

Live agents wanted.

Write for Catalogue and Terms.

The Thomas Auto-Bi Co.
1442 Niagara Street
Buffalo, N. Y.

A Henderson "4" ad of 1912.

MotorCycling   March 28, 1912.

Ask Her which way she would rather ride.   Then write for
booklet telling all about the quiet, vibrationless, flexible, powerful,
sweet running

HENDERSON

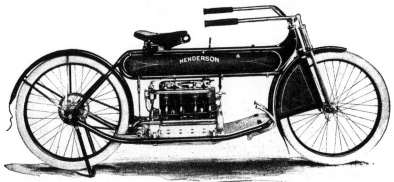

4 Cyl.   7 H. P. $325

**Dealers—The Henderson will not conflict with the singles and
twins you are now handling. It will simply complete your line**

HENDERSON MOTORCYCLE CO.
268 Jefferson Ave.   -   -   Detroit, Mich.

189

There were many different designs and models of early motorcycles as shown here, including the Curtiss and Marvel built by pioneer aviator, Glenn H. Curtiss. Other ads offered unique accessories, such as tandems, methods of converting a bicycle into a motorbike, rear wheel locks; there were "Buy it Wholesale" ads, and even a time payment plan by the makers of the Peerless. At right is the once popular Rogers Sidecar, distributed by Irving Beck, founder of the Beck Corporation (now importers and manufacturers of motorcycle and imported car parts and accessories).

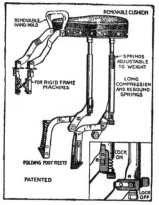

November 1912

SOME PROMINENT ENGLISH MOTORCYCLISTS

Mr. George Bernard Shaw

Sir David Bruce
(From a photograph taken in C. Africa)

Rev. E. P. Greenhill.
(Chairman Competition Committee – A-C.U.)

Mr. C. J. Burnup.

Prince Francois de Bourbon.

Rev. P. W. Bischoff.

Rear Admiral Sir R. K. Arbuthnot.

Mr. A. V. Roe.

Mr. Tom Sopwith.

Sir Arthur Conan Doyle

Mr. Stanley S. Leonard
(The new English Tenor)

Mr. John Ball.

*Herb Royston, antique car and
motorcycle buff, shown on
his 1911 Excelsior.*

*Stunt riding on a stage. Bike is a
1911 Indian single. 4 h.p.*

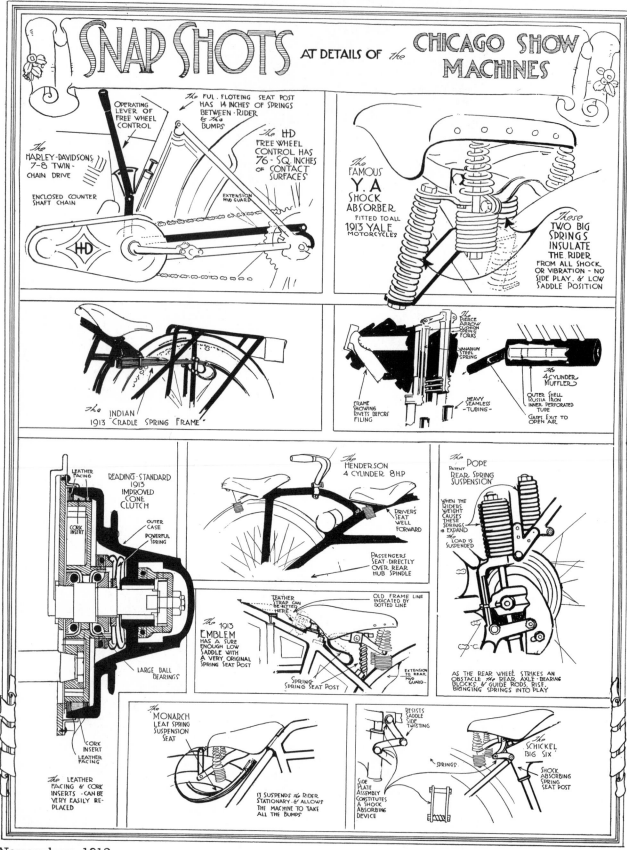

November 1912

194

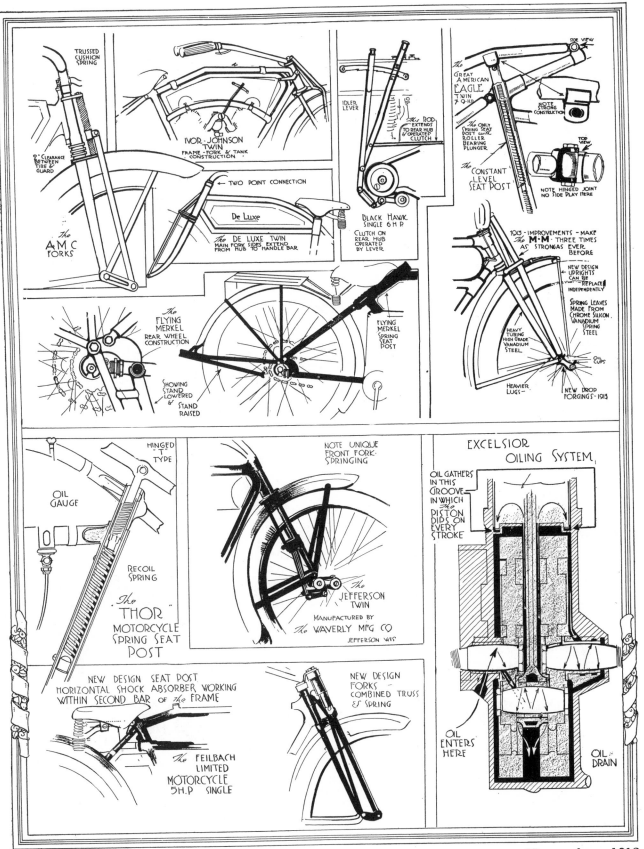

November 1912

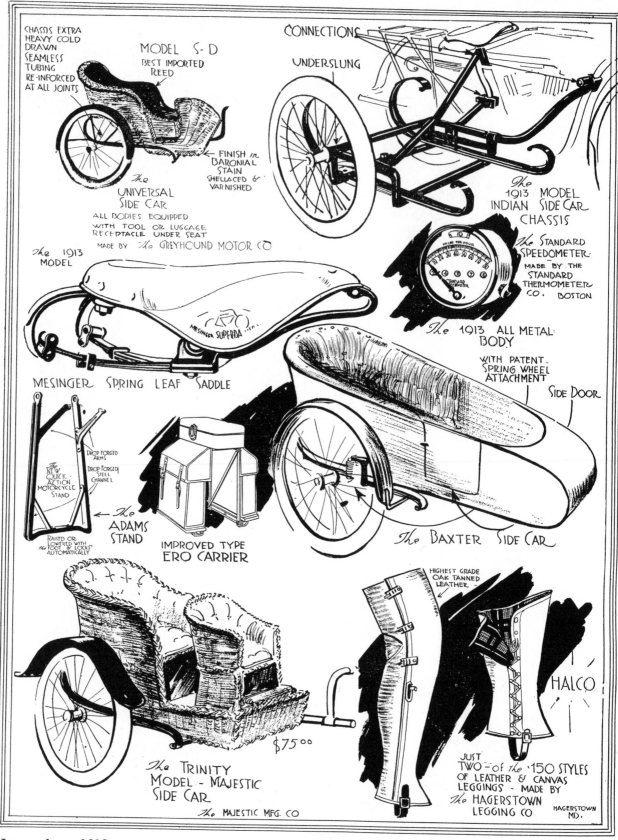

CHASSIS EXTRA HEAVY COLD DRAWN SEAMLESS TUBING RE-INFORCED AT ALL JOINTS

MODEL S-D
BEST IMPORTED REED

CONNECTIONS

UNDERSLUNG

FINISH in BARONIAL STAIN SHELLACED & VARNISHED

The UNIVERSAL SIDE CAR

ALL BODIES EQUIPPED WITH TOOL OR LUGGAGE RECEPTACLE UNDER SEAT

MADE BY The GREYHOUND MOTOR CO

The 1913 MODEL INDIAN SIDE CAR CHASSIS

The Standard SPEEDOMETER MADE BY THE STANDARD THERMOMETER CO. BOSTON

The 1913 MODEL

MESINGER SUPERBA

MESINGER SPRING LEAF SADDLE

The 1913 ALL METAL BODY

WITH PATENT SPRING WHEEL ATTACHMENT

SIDE DOOR

The NEW QUICK ACTION MOTORCYCLE STAND

DROP FORGED ARMS

DROP FORGED STEEL CHANNEL

The ADAMS STAND

RAISED OR LOWERED WITH The FOOT & LOCKS AUTOMATICALLY

IMPROVED TYPE ERO CARRIER

The BAXTER SIDE CAR

HIGHEST GRADE OAK TANNED LEATHER

HALCO

$75.00

The TRINITY MODEL - MAJESTIC SIDE CAR

The MAJESTIC MFG. CO

JUST TWO of the 150 STYLES OF LEATHER & CANVAS LEGGINGS - MADE BY The HAGERSTOWN LEGGING CO

HAGERSTOWN MD.

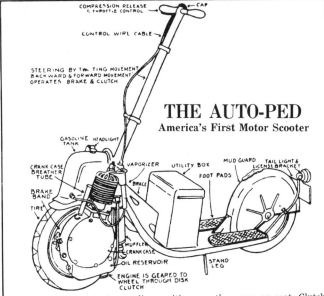

THE AUTO-PED
America's First Motor Scooter

The operator rode in standing position . . . there was no seat. Clutch and brake were operated by moving handle bar lever back and forth. Lighting was by flywheel generator. Front wheel drive engine was 2 H.P. and the machine would do 35 miles an hour. It was built by Auto-Ped Co. of America, New York, prior to the first world war.

HARLEY-DAVIDSON

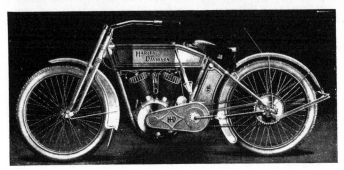

700 Used by One Corporation

The Cyclone was a popular early-day make used for street and racing. It had an overhead camshaft engine, and Cyclone riders won many important events.

AMERICA'S FIRST SCOOTER. 1915. *The operator rode in standing position—there was no seat. Clutch and brake were operated by moving handlebar lever back and forth. Lighting was by flywheel generator. Front wheel drive engine has 2 h.p. and the machine would do 35 miles an hour. It was built by Auto-Ped Co. of America, New York, prior to the First World War.*

Motorcycle Relay Riders on Their Way

Dispatch bearers rushing across the country with President Wilson's message to the Mayor of San Francisco. Rain or shine, night and day, in good going and bad, intrepid riders will demonstrate for the War Department the value of the motorcycle as a means of rapid communication, which fact has already been demonstrated to the European countries.

CHICAGO, July 16—President Wilson's message to the Mayor of San Francisco, will be rushing across the country via motorcycle relay by the time this issue of MotorCycling & Bicycling is in the hands of most of our readers.

Chairman John L. Donovan of the F. A. M. competition committee, who has charge of the arrangements for this signal demonstration of motorcycle utility, will leave Chicago, Saturday, to go over the route on all relays west of Chicago, and hold a final consultation with each manager. He has arranged his train schedule to give him about half an hour at each relay point, and expects to beat the message into Sacramento, but a very short delay is likely to upset his calculations and the riders may have the added glory of beating the relay manager across the country despite the fact that he travels by train and has a three day start out of Chicago.

Wilson to Deliver Message

President Wilson has promised that he will hand the message in person to the dispatch bearer who rides the first relay out of Washington. It will be placed in a special leather dispatch case and strapped over the shoulder of the bearer. Two other riders will escort him so that in event of mishap or delay of any kind the message will not be halted. Should the dispatch bearer stop for any reason the case will be snatched by one of the escorting riders and kept moving. This plan will be followed for the entire distance except in some of the mountainous territory in the west where riders are not so easily obtained.

"Getting There" the Thing

While the difficult roads may in a measure slow up the time they will have their useful lesson which will probably be just as valuable to the motorcycle industry as the speed made on the better going. It is the purpose of the Trade Journals which have promoted this great demonstration of motorcycle adaptability to arouse the interest of the entire country in motor-

cycles, not only as a speedy means of travel but as a stable, rapid and dependable method of getting from one end of the country to the other. Therefore, the greater speed possible on the good going will be just as valuable but no more valuable than the slower time on the bad going. Its the "getting there" despite all adverse conditions that will count. The riders who have good going must depend on their speed for their glory. Those who encounter mud and rocks and sand and mountains will get their glory in getting through, not at 60 miles an hour perhaps, but at a third of it or even less, overcoming all obstacles and winning through.

Rain or Shine, Night and Day

Night and day, rain or shine the message will be kept going. If it is not cloudy the moon will be out most of the nights but whether it is bright moonlight or pitch dark there will be no halt. From the time the message leaves President Wilson's hand at 10 o'clock Monday morning until it is turned over to the Mayor of San

Francisco early Saturday morning nothing that can be foreseen will be allowed to interfere with its progress.

At the San Francisco fair grounds a great map eight feet long has been erected. Across this the route of the relay riders has is plainly marked and as the message travels from point to point its progress will be shown by a moving figure of a motorcycle rider which will travel across the map, thus keeping the thousands of exposition visitors posted.

Speed Limits Waved

From east to west the country across, relay managers have been busy for weeks, arranging all the little details that make for success. Local riders familiar with the ground over which they are to travel, have been chosen as far as practicable. Where this was not possible the relay riders have been on the ground long enough in advance to go at least once over the route. Erwin G. Baker, who is to ride several of the mountain relays in the west, has several times negotiated these trails and knows them perhaps better than any other rider in the country. In most of the towns and cities through which the riders pass, the speed limit has been waived and in addition special police protection has been promised to keep the route clear of traffic while the riders are passing. In many cities escorts of local riders will be provided to guide the dispatch bearers through town so that no time need be lost because of a mistake in the way.

Chief of Police Healy, of Chicago, has agreed to furnish an escort of motorcycle policemen for the relay riders in and out of the city, to insure that their progress is not interfered with. Mayor Thompson, of Chicago, will send a message of his own to the Mayor of San Francisco, and it will be carried in the case with that of President Wilson's.

Chas. Essing, manager of the Sportsman's club, will act as Chicago host. First Assistant Chief of Police Scheuttler will lead the riders in and out of Chicago, in the Big Tom fire auto, with siren screaming all the way.

Keep in Touch by Wire

An elaborate system of telegraphic information has been arranged for. When the first relay leaves Washington a wire will be sent to the second relay at Baltimore to get ready. Baltimore will in turn notify Philadelphia that the message has left Washington. When the message reaches Baltimore Philadelphia will be notified to get ready and will notify New York that the message has left Baltimore. By this means the relay points, two relays ahead of the message, will be kept informed of its progress and so have their

---

EACH RELAY is the MOST IMPORTANT.

It is up to every relay manager and rider to DO HIS UTMOST.

The failure of one relay might disarrange the entire schedule and detract greatly from the success of this big enterprise which means so much to the motorcycle industry in the United States.

The press of the country has given much space to the ocean to ocean rush. INTENSE PUBLIC INTEREST HAS BEEN AROUSED.

All across the country PEOPLE ARE WATCHING for telegraphic reports of the progress of the message which President Wilson entrusted to the dispatch riders Monday morning.

Let each rider and each relay manager make himself individually responsible for the success of his part in the relay so that when the race is done there will have been NO WEAK SPOTS AND NO REGRETS, but, instead, general satisfaction to everybody for having taken a creditable part in a wonderful demonstration of the stability and reliability of motorcycles and the courage and resourcefulness of motorcycle riders. GO TO IT!!

---

starters ready to grab the message case and start without an instant's delay.

Better Roads in East

Eastern riders will probably have better roads than those west of Chicago. The unusual rains in the central west have made the going almost impassable in many places. This will provide an additional test for the mettle of both men and machines. In many cases it is expected that the riders will take to the railroad tracks, making the best time they can through the cinders and over the ties. It will be a case of any way to get there but get there some way and lose no time about it.

Sanctioned by War Department

The United States Department of War has sanctioned the attempt of the motorcycle riders to make better time from New York to San Francisco than is made by ordinary mail trains and Secretary Garrison has taken great interest in the pre-

Riding the Ties

liminary plans. Over in Europe the motorcycle has daily demonstrated its superiority over other methods of dispatch service in times of war. American motorcycles, be-

cause of their greater power and strength are largely used by the European armies. What can be done in Europe can also be done in America. One of the primary ideas back of the relay is to demonstrate to the United States War Department the real worth of the motorcycle in dispatch service.

The Riders

The riders so far as announced follow:

Relay A—Fred M. Mills, manager; Frank S. Long, L. S. Leishaar, J. Seabrook, riders.

Relay B—William Wood, manager; John V. Daniels, Clifford Gibbs, Edward Hance, riders.

Relay C—C. D. Feiler, manager; Arthur Chapple, Robert Kennick, riders.

Relay 1—Stanley T. Kellogg, manager; William F. Stubner, Ben Willig, Orrin Perry, riders.

Relay 2—George Sorensen, manager; George Sorensen, Howard Booth, Thos F. Ryan, riders.

Relay 3—A. P. Strogonoff, manager; A. P. Strogonoff, Thomas Ryan, A. Holzhaner, riders.

Relay 4—Utica Cycle Co., manager; Stewart J. Baird, Charles Fink, Frank J. Bowen, riders.

Relay 5—P. L. Adams, manager; P. L. Adams, C. F. Chase, C. S. Ripley, riders.

Relay 6—Geo. M. Spacher, manager; Geo. M. Spacher, A. K. Chalmers, Wm. Pergrem, riders.

Relay 7—William Schack, manager; William Schack, John Warwick, riders.

Relay 8—John Wilk, manager; Ralph Lossie, Roger Brandt, Archie Mong, riders.

Relay 9—E. H. Tracy, manager; C. L. Murray, D. M. Pollock, Clover Friedman, Ivan Jacobs, riders.

Relay 10—Charles Oberwegner, manager; A. R. Oberwegner, Roy Carns, Henry Rosenbloom, riders.

Relay 11—James Ash, manager; Maldwyn Jones, C. F. Pineau, Gibson, riders.

Relay 12—J. P. Wood, manager; J. P. Wood, Don Johns, Korn, riders.

Relay 13—Aurora Automatic Co., manager; Ed J. Hawkins, Harry Sawyer, Geo. Heutasel, riders.

Relay 14—Roy R. Baer, manager; Elmer Abbott, Walter Loos, Arthur Lowman, riders.

Relay 15—Streed & Sheppers, manager; John C. Swanson, Phil Swanson, August Scheppers, riders.

Relay 16—Carl Larson, manager; W. M. Thul, Vern Soderberg, Carl Larson, riders.

Relay 17—Spring Hub Bicycle Mfg. Co., manager; Ben Peterson, F. F. Oliver, George Cooke, riders.

Relay 18—W. E. Dewey, manager; W. E.

Dewey, Carl Munkers, Otto Ramor, riders.

Relay 19—The Nebraska Cycle Co., manager; Hugo Heyn, Lloyd Jensen, John Strehle, riders.

Relay 20—L. E. Parsons, manager; Oscar Olson, F. R. Goodwin, L. E. Parsons, riders.

Relay 21—S. S. Nicholls, manager; S. S. Nicholls, Elmer Merrimee, C. O. Pulver, riders..

Relay 22—Ralph W. Vroman, manager; Walter N. Nelson, James R. Green, C. F. Williams, riders.

Relay 23—Floyd Clymer, manager; Floyd Clymer, Frank Kunce, Ellis McDill, riders.

Relay 24—George Wales, manager; George Wales, Walter J. Reichen, David Stalker, riders.

Relay 25—George Wales, manager; George Wales, Walter J. Reichen, David Stalker, riders.

Relay 26—C. L. Bunten, manager; C. L. Bunten, George O'Brien, riders.

Relay 27—W. D. Rishell, manager; William Moore, Harry Wood, Peter Johnson, riders.

Relay 28—W. D. Rishell, manager; Norman Hopper, rider.

Relay 28a—J. Lewis Anderson, manager; Niel Nielsen, George O. Rice, J. L. Anderson, riders.

Relay 29—Ray Shurtiff, manager; Don Smith, Ray Peck, Rink Smurthwait, riders.

Relay 30—W. R. Rishell, manager; William Moore, Harry Wood, Peter Johnson, riders.

Relay 31—Lon Claflin, manager; Lon Claflin, A. S. Margetts, riders.

Relay 32—Erwin G. Baker, rider and manager.

Relay 33—Erwin G. Baker, manager; Erwin G. Baker, Robert Hermann, Walter Tesch, riders.

Relay 34—Erwin G. Baker, manager and rider.

Relay 35—C. McQuerry, manager; Vernon Summerfield, Laruitz Lund, C. McQuerry, riders.

Relay 36—Mack Auto Co., manager; Archie Swan, Frank Golden, W. C. Gill, riders.

Relay 37—E. O. Putzman, manager; Dutch Fabian, R. K. Bowman, A. Turnbull, riders.

Relay 38—J. Fink, manager; W. Snider, J. F. Whitman, George Barton, riders.

Relay 38—L. S. Upson, manager; A. Chelini, G. L. Budd, E. H. Rueter, riders.

Will they beat Donovan across the country?

An artist's conception of Federation of American Motorcyclist's competition chairman, John L. Donavon, on the rear end of a train. The train won, due to delays caused by heavy rains and gumbo mud across Illinois, Iowa and Nebraska.

No time lost

An artist's conception of Floyd Clymer and Frank Kunce delivering the pouch to George Wales, on the fly, as 2,000 spectators watched the transfer on Carey Avenue in Cheyenne, Wyoming.

PONY EXPRESS

In 1915 John L. Donovan, F.A.M. Competition Chairman, conceived the idea of a re-enactment of the early Pony Express days. President Wilson sent a letter to the president of the Pan-Pacific Exposition. Riders of different makes who best knew their respective states and highways (what a joke! they were only dirt roads or trails in many regions); usually two or three men made up the team, so in the event of a breakdown there was a reserve to carry on. Note, however, that "Cannonball" Baker alone carried the message in three relays. On No. 33 he had two others with him, but in Relays 32 and 34 he was both man and rider. He took the train between relays and was selected because he then knew more of the roads and routes than any other rider. On Relay No. 23 Frank Kunce and I rode Excelsiors. We waited at Big Springs, Nebr. three days for the riders from the East to reach us. Heavy rains and gumbo mud in Illinois, Iowa and Nebraska delayed the riders' arrival in San Francisco.

Kunce and I (McDill, a third rider, did not show up) averaged 35 miles an hour over rutted roads, with weeds and sunflowers often hitting our hands on the bars. In some places we often rode with our feet dangling above the footboards, which sometimes were so low they hit the sides of the sandy or dirt ruts.

At Cheyenne, Wyoming, before a crowd of 2,000 people along Carey Avenue, we handed the message pouch to Geo. Wales, Relay 24 manager. His riders left Cheyenne at 6:00 P.M., rode all night over the Continental Divide Mountains, arriving at Laramie (60 miles from Cheyenne) at 6:00 A.M. the next morning.

The message was delivered at San Francisco just four days, 21 hours late—but we got there. What a deal that was!

Four Solid Carloads of
Motorcycles and Sidecars
—for FLOYD CLYMER

They Are EXCELSIORS and INDIANS "of Course"

THIS IS THE LAGEST NUMBER OF GASOLINE PROPELLED VEHICLES EVER SHIPPED INTO THE ROCKY MOUNTAIN REGION—IN NUMBER, IT WOULD REQUIRE MORE THAN A TRAINLOAD OF THE AVERAGE CARLOADS OF AUTOMOBILES TO EQUAL THIS SHIPMENT—IT IS, BY FAR, THE LARGEST SHIPMENT OF MOTORCYCLES EVER SHIPPED TO ANY POINT BETWEEN CHICAGO AND THE PACIFIC COAST.

"1919 INDIAN"

THE INCREASING DEMAND FOR MOTORCYCLES, ESPECIALLY THE INDIAN AND EXCELSIOR, PROMPTED US TO ORDER THIS LARGE SHIPMENT. THIS WILL ENABLE US TO DELIVER PROMPTLY ANY MODEL OF EITHER OF THESE POPULAR MOTORCYCLES

70,000 MOTORCYCLES were ordered by Uncle Sam for military use during the war. Motorcycles and sidecars were used in every army camp in America and on every battlefield of Europe.

The war has demonstrated to thousands that the modern Motorcycle and Sidecar cannot be compared for a moment with any automobile, regardless of price or horse power, when it comes to economy, power, reliability and superior ability to negotiate the worst of roads under any and all conditions.

"MODEL 19 EXCELSIOR"

The Indian
Built by the LARGEST MANUFACTURERS OF MO-TORCYCLES IN THE WORLD. UNCLE SAM'S CHOICE, proven by the fact that 60 per cent of all Motor-cycles ordered for military purposes were INDIANS.
Out of a total of 70,000 Motorcycles ordered, 40,000 were INDIANS.
The last order called for 28,000 Motorcycles, and 18,000 INDIANS were specified, or NEARLY TWICE AS MANY AS THE NEAREST COMPETITIVE MAKE.
The following OFFICIAL WORLD'S RECORDS ARE HELD BY THE INDIAN:
WORLD'S 24-hour record (both heavyweight and lightweight classes).
WORLD'S 24-hour record with sidecar outfit.
WORLD'S 500 and 1,000-mile records.
WORLD'S 12-hour record (solo).
WORLD'S 12-hour record (sidecar).
Practically every WORLD'S AMATEUR RECORD.

The Excelsior
We have handled the EXCELSIOR so long that we feel that it needs no introduction.
TWICE AS MANY EXCELSIORS WERE SOLD IN COLORADO DURING 1918 AS THE NEAREST COMPETITIVE MAKE.
The following OFFICIAL WORLD'S RECORDS ARE HELD BY THE EXCELSIOR:
WORLD'S 200-MILE RECORD.
WORLD'S 300-MILE RECORD (AMERICAN NATIONAL CHAMPIONSHIP).
WORLD'S ECONOMY RECORD, 128 miles on one gallon of gasoline.
FOR THE PAST TWO YEARS WINNER OF THE WORLD'S CHAMPIONSHIP HILL CLIMB HELD AT CAPISTRANO, CALIF.
PIKES PEAK RECORD and numerous other records.

Purchasers of Indian and Excelsior Motorcycles are assured of real service, as our stock of Motorcycle Parts and Accessories is larger than any other Motorcycle establishment in the West.
MOTORCYCLE RIDERS WHO ARE IN NEED OF PARTS AND ACCES-SORIES WILL FIND THAT WE ARE VERY PROMPT AND THAT MAIL OR-DERS ARE FILLED SAME DAY AS RECEIVED.

We also have a fine line of used and rebuilt machines that are priced very low.
Write for our latest bulletin and literature describing the 1919 models.
Any of our Motorcycles can be purchased on the easy payment plan.
We have some fine territory open for good, live dealers, and if interested write us re-garding our agency proposition for your territory.
We invite you to call and inspect the new models.

FLOYD CLYMER "LARGEST MOTORCYCLE DEALER IN THE WEST"

—— TWO STORES ——

1336 Broadway, Denver, Colo.   NEW BRANCH STORE OPENS MAY FIRST AT STERLING, COLO.   1012 Eighth Ave., Greeley, Colo.

This is a reduction of a full page ad by the author, which appeared in the Denver Post, Denver News and the Greeley Tribune.

U.S. Army motorcycles. In World War I, the U.S. Army used motorcycles, many with side cars. Thousands of Indians and Harley-Davidsons were purchased by the U.S. Army. (Opposite page)

Board track racing prior to 1915. Board track racing was popular. There were tracks in many cities, and they were circular—usually 1/4 to 1/2 mile distances. (Below)

Remember When . . .

. . . there were motorcycle races in Shorewood?

SHOREWOOD was still known as East Milwaukee when the Milwaukee Motordrome opened on Oakland and Newton avs. in 1913. The track, built next to the old Ravenna park, was one-fourth of a mile at the pole line (four laps to a mile) and banked at an angle of 58 degrees. Wednesday, Saturday and Sunday evenings were race nights with such noted motorcycle riders at Glenn Stokes, "Red" Parkhurst and Jack Doyle raising cheers from their fans as they got off to a flying start and raced around and around. Spectators were politely requested not to lean on the railing or throw anything on the track, p l e a s e, but cheers, whistles, hooting and hollering w e r e appreciated. (Picture from cover of the Official Program, Sunday, July 20, 1913, Milwaukee Motordrome, in the local history room, Milwaukee public library.)

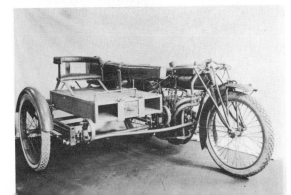

Indian once had a self starter — a Hendee Special — about 1912; prior to that they had a hand cranked model, a 2-speed DeLuxe job.

*　　*　　*

Harley-Davidson once used a two-speed and a clutch in the rear hub. In 1913, their first chain driven single was called "5-35" — "5" for H.P. and "35" for cubic inch displacement.

*　　*　　*

Spring frames were once popular on American motorcycles — Merkel, Pope and Indian used them. Merkel had two enclosed coil springs in the upper frame tube. Pope had open coil springs at the end of the frame. Indian used a leaf spring on each side of the frame.

*　　*　　*

Most early motorcycles had a drip oiler. Turn the valve and the oil dripped through a glass. One early make, the Thomas Auto-Bi, advertised that you could "oil the machine without dismounting." SOME feature!

*　　*　　*

Dual valve engines were once used by both Indian and Harley-Davidson in their racing machines. Both makes had a four-valve single and an eight-valve twin overhead. Indian used valves of different sizes, and they were in a flat head. Harley-Davidson used a roof overhead similar to their present 61 o.h.v. design, excepting that four valves per cylinder were used. The singles were

Twin Cylinder Model 17

Motor—Air cooled, piston displacement not exceeding 61 cu. in. Mechanical construction to meet any requirements.

Tanks—Any shape, size or location desirable.

Lubrication—Hand pump or mechanical pump, either or both, or any oiling system deemed advisable for the safety or convenience of the rider.

Wheels—28 in.

Tires—28x3 in. or smaller.

Saddle—Troxel or special racing.

Transmission—Roller chain.

Ignition—Magneto.

Wheel Base—51½ in. or optional.

Clutch, brake, forks, handlebars, frame, finish and equipment optional.

The right is reserved to change any feature without further notice, whether listed above or not.

Price, $1500 F. O. B. Milwaukee

30-50 Single Cylinder

Price, $1400 F. O. B. Milwaukee

In 1916-17 $1,500.00 would buy this "works" Harley-Davidson racer, the same as used by Janke and Clymer in the 300-mile International Race at Dodge City, Kans. But, even so, Harley-Davidson selected their customers. Just every Joe Doakes could not get delivery— a clever way of saying "no soap."

There is no more thrilling sport than 1/2-mile dirt-track racing. Shown here is a meet at South Bend, Indiana, with riders broadsiding into the first corner.

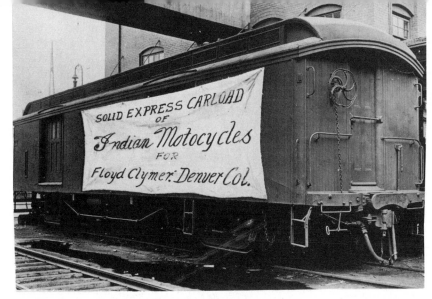

In 1920, during a freight embargo, the first carload of motorcycles ever to be shipped by express were sent from the Indian factory in Springfield, Mass. to Denver, Colo. They were Scout and Chief models. Express charges averaged $24.12 per unit, as against $11.20 by freight.

used mostly on half-mile tracks, the twins on mile and larger tracks and speedways.

* * *

Excelsior once built an overhead twin racing machine, and also tried out an overhead camshaft job.

* * *

In early days "Cannonball" Baker made a fortune riding motorcycles across the U.S. for records. He rode at various times Indian, Ace, Nearcar. Later he drove Cadillac, Templar, Franklin, Jewett, Crosley and other cars across country for records.

* * *

Few know that the front-wheel brake on a motorcycle was first used on the Wilkinson Motorcycle built in 1911 in London, England. It was operated by a handlebar lever, and in appearance was similar to conventional design.

* * *

Thor engines were used by many of the first makers of motorcycles in America, including Indian and Reading-Standard.

* * *

Reading-Standard, built in early days at Reading, Pennsylvania, had an advertising slogan "Built and tested in the mountains." Competitors used to change it to "Built in the mountains and tested down hill!" It was a good machine in its day.

Ab Jenkins, former Salt Lake City Mayor and holder of the world's long distance speed records in the Mormon "Meteor" on the salt beds of Bonneville, Utah, was once a motorcycle racer. Ab owned and raced Excelsiors in Utah and Idaho in 1912 and 1913. He was especially good on half-mile dirt tracks. Ab was only one of the many famous car drivers and aviators who secured his early speed experience on motorcycles.

* * *

Henderson brothers, Tom and Will, were automobile manufacturers before they started building motorcycles in Detroit. They were related to Alexander Winton, builder of the early Winton car. They later sold out to Schwinn of Excelsior and soon retired from the motorcycle field. Will was killed in an accident.

* * *

Glenn Curtiss, pioneer airman, once built motorcycles. A single and a twin were made at Hammondsport, New York. He is accredited with a mile in 28 seconds on a special 8-cylinder motorcycle on the Florida beach. Many people doubt that he ever made such fast time.

* * *

Pierce of Buffalo, New York, once built a belt-driven single and a 4-cylinder motorcycle. The four was a "T" head design, unit power plant. The first models were one-speed and later on they had

Shown here is a special Indian Twin of 1920, manufactured for competition in England. It was known as a TT model. Note the front stand and license plate on the front fender, and the low English-type racing bars. (Top)

This exhibit, at the National Western Stock Show, in Denver, Colorado, features a War Model Cleveland, Indian side car unit with a machine gun. Similar units were used in World War I by the Army. At right are a cut-away Excelsior, and a Powerplus model Indian twin. (Opposite, top)

Motorcycle hill climbs were always popular, especially in the 1920's. Shown here is the famous Capistrano Hill in California. Rider on the Indian is the author who was the first to top this famous hill without the use of tractor band on the rear wheel. (Opposite, bottom)

two speeds. Contrary to general belief, they were not fast, and had but little power. Most any good single would beat them on the level or uphill. The oil and gasoline were carried in the frame tubes, which were quite large in diameter. Not a bad idea at that. The design still has possibilities.

*   *   *

Harley-Davidson Motor Company, originally consisting of Arthur Davidson and William Harley, later joined by William and Walter Davidson, has been one of the notable and successful firms in the United States, owned entirely by a closed group, the founders. No stock was ever sold to the public.

*   *   *

In the late 1880's a German immigrant named Ignaz Schwinn came to America. He brazed bicycle frames for $3.50 a day. Working night and day, he later purchased material with his savings. He sold Montgomery Ward and Butler Brothers bicycles to be made under their trade names. He bought the Excelsior Supply Company, became manufacturer of Excelsior Motorcycles, and later added the Henderson. In 1931 he closed out the motorcycle business. Retiring to his first love, the bicycle, the business prospered. The Schwinn bicycle is world famous. Most of the popular innovations such as balloon tires, front wheel brake, spring fork and others have come from the House of Schwinn.

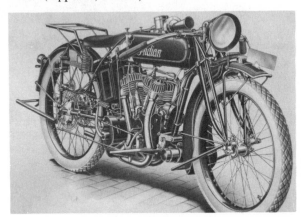

One of the famous riders was Ralph Hepburn, who was a member of the Indian and Harley-Davidson teams. Hepburn was also a famous race car driver. He was killed in practice in qualifying trials at the Indianapolis Speedway in 1948. (Bottom)

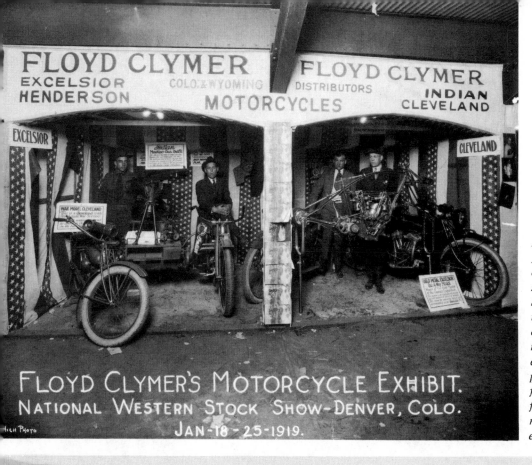

FLOYD CLYMER
EXCELSIOR   COLO.&WYOMING   DISTRIBUTORS   FLOYD CLYMER
HENDERSON   MOTORCYCLES   INDIAN
                                                CLEVELAND

EXCELSIOR   CLEVELAND

FLOYD CLYMER'S MOTORCYCLE EXHIBIT.
NATIONAL WESTERN STOCK SHOW–DENVER, COLO.
JAN-18-25-1919.

In 1920 there was an embargo on freight shipments, so this carload of 40 Indian Chiefs and Scouts was shipped from the Indian factory in Springfield, Mass. to Denver. At that time it was the largest, and the only shipment of a carload of motorcycles, via express. In those days, before motor trucks or airplanes, most shipments were by freight. It took 10 days by freight, four days by express. Cost per machine $27.00, as against $12.50 each by freight.

Two famous early day speedway (short track) champions: George Lannom and "Sprouts" Elder shown in 1932.

Carroll Resweber is honored by a group of civic and A.M.A. officials in his home town of Cedarburg, Wis. for winning No. 1 A.M.A. championship position in 1960.

Joe Leonard, many times A.M.A. National Champion, shown on his Harley-Davidson at Sacramento, Calif. in 1961, where he won the 25-mile national title. Presenting trophy, at left, is California Lt. Gov. Glenn Anderson, a former motorcyclist and racing machine owner, Mrs. Anderson, A.M.A. Secretary Lin Kuchler; and promoter J. C. Agajanian is on the right.

The Harley-Davidson racing team at Dodge City 300-mile F.A.M. Dirt Track Championship. Taken about 1920.

THE REVIVAL OF
U.S. ROAD RACING

It is good to see a revival of motorcycle road racing in the United States. Road racing was once popular in American motorcycle racing history. Some of the best known and most interesting motorcycle events held in the early days of competition were the famous races usually held over country roads before the advent of the modern highway.

Probably the most interesting and well-known of the early road races were the Elgin, Illinois, and Savannah, Georgia road races. The Elgin race was also once a prominent annual automobile road racing event. These contests were long-distance events, and the competing machines were 61-cubic-inch twins, most of them having single speed drives with only a clutch or compensating sprocket between the engine and the rear wheel. Later on two-speed machines were used at Elgin, when such famous riders as "Cannonball" Baker, Charles Balke and Les Taylor were the stars of Indian, and Bob Perry and Carl Goudy were the Excelsior Aces. Other famous riders were Bill Brier and Shorty Matthews, who rode Thors. Average speeds were between 60 and 70 miles per hour.

Savannah, Georgia, was the home of motorcycle road racing for many years. These events attracted national attention and were held on public highways. It was in the last days of Savannah road racing that the present-day popular and capable rider, Ed Kretz (as a practically unknown rider from the West Coast) won surprising victories.

The Harley-Davidson racing team,
and the start of the 300-mile-F.A.M.
Championship at Dodge City,
Kansas, about 1920.

This unique Flexi Sidecar was used by many sidecar racing men, including Floyd Dreyer and "Jiggs" Price. This Indian combination was used quite successfully by early day racing star, "Shrimp" Burns, kneeling alongside the unit.

La Grande, Oregon, was also the home of some motorcycle racing events on country roads, and the famous road races of Marion, Indiana, attracted attention for some years. These events were held on the very narrow Indiana roads which were common at that time. I shall never forget competing in the first 200-mile Marion road race in which the stars of the respective factories took part. It was like riding on a road that actually had just about enough room for one automobile in the center of the road, and there were four rather sharp corners.

Among the most interesting of early American road racing events were the desert classics, such as the races across the desert through sand and sage brush. These events were held from San Diego to Phoenix, El Paso to Phoenix, and Los Angeles to Phoenix, and were the outgrowth of some of the early day automobile contests which were held over the same roads.

Most famous of all road races on the Pacific Coast was the Venice road race held in the "City by the Sea" near Los Angeles. The riders raced over what are now prominent streets of Venice, and factory support was given by the major factories such as Harley-Davidson (who were the winners), Indian, Excelsior, and a sprinkling of riders representing other makes. The machines used in these events were 61-cubic-inch twins with three-speed transmission and magneto ignition.

There were also many cross-country events in the days before the law interfered too much with motorcyclists seeking to gain fame (but no fortune) in establishing records across country and between cities. The coast to coast records events might well be called road races — however, they were against time. Most outstanding and best known coast to coast champion is the old war horse, Erwin G. "Cannonball" Baker. These early events and cross-country records were sanctioned by the Federation of American Motorcyclists, which was a similar organization to the American Motorcycle Association of recent years.

Baker established many coast to coast records in both directions, and in each instance Baker's record did not usually stand for long, for there were such famous road riders as Roy Artley, Allan Bedell, Wells Bennett and Hap Scherer among the early cross-country Aces who made life miserable for the "Cannonball." Baker not only established many motorcycle cross-country records, but he also made some records for leading automobile factories. "Bake," always a shrewd negotiator, usually induced Frank Weschler to back him with high bonuses if he beat previous records. Weschler was the Indian "chief" who in those days had control of the purse strings at Indian and at that time the moneybags at Indian contained real "coin of the realm." Baker usually had an agreement with Indian that they would pay him so much money for every hour — in the real early days it was for every day — and in later days for every hour and minute that he knocked off the previous record. At one time, about 1915, Baker was so far ahead of the previous record at Williams, Arizona, that Indian would have had to pay him about $20,000 had he continued his schedule to Los Angeles. Unfortunately, near

Williams, Arizona, Baker had a spill resulting in a broken leg that ended his chances for the big money.

Three-flag records were always popular on the West Coast, and these records were made from the Canadian border, across the United States, to the Mexican border near Tijuana, Old Mexico. Baker also competed in these events, although probably the most outstanding rider to hold the record most of the time was the late Roy Artley who at different times had ridden Hendersons and Harley-Davidsons. Wells Bennett, an Excelsior long-distance Ace, also held the record several times, as did Hap Scherer on a 37-cubic-inch Harley-Davidson opposed middleweight twin, known as a sport model.

As better highways came into general use and more efficient police patrolling of the highways, these famous three-flag road races were abandoned.

During my competition career I established two long-distance road records from Chicago to Denver, and from Denver to Chicago. In one instance I rode a Model K 4-cylinder Henderson, making the run in 54 hours between Chicago and Denver, some of it over Iowa gumbo roads that were deep with mud. I recall one record I held just nine days when Hap Scherer on a little 37-cubic-inch sport-model Harley-Davidson twin knocked my record into a cocked hat.

I also remember the early road races held in and around Denver. In one instance I raced from Denver to Cheyenne and back, through Greeley, over rough narrow roads, and I had the complete

The Harley-Davidson Enthusia

Published now and then by the Harley-Davidson Motor Co., Milwaukee, U. S. A.   Not published n

No. 4

Irving Janke, a Milwaukee boy and a Milwaukee motorcycle, the Dodge City Champions

All Dodge City Records Are Captured by the Harley-Davidsons

1st Irving Janke, Harley-Davidson	. . . . .	3:45:3(
2nd Joe Wolter, _____	. . . .	3:47:5:
3rd Ray Weishaar, Harley-Davidson	. . .	3:55:5:
4th "Speck" Warner, _____	. . . . .	4:16:1:
5th Gene Walker, _____	. . . .	4:20:4!
6th "Morty" Graves, _____	. . . .	4:22:1

100-Mile—Floyd Clymer, Harley-Davidson . . 1:11:4!
   Averaging 83.62 miles an hour, beating Goudy's record by : minutes, 25 seconds.

200-Mile—Irving Janke, Harley-Davidson . . . 2:27:5!
   Averaging 81.47 miles an hour, beating Walker's record by ! minutes, 36 seconds.

300-Mile—Irving Janke, Harley-Davidson . . . 3:45.3(
   Averaging 79.79 miles an hour, beating Walker's record by 1(minutes, 9 seconds.

Harley-Davidson Wins Dodge City Classic Again This Year

JULY fourth this year certainly was a rip snorting holiday for Harley-Davidson speed fans. During the week following the national holiday we were deluged with telegrams and letters from dealers all over the country. "They all inhaled Harley-Davidson smoke," was the striking phrase gleaned from a wire sent by C. F. Braunlich & Co., Wheeling, W. Va., that fittingly described the speed activities of the Gray Fellow on the fourth.

"Wire results Dodge City," came in from everywhere and demonstrated the unusual interest manifested by dealers and riders in the annual 300-mile classic of the Kansas prairies. And they were not disappointed. Of course, it was hardly to be expected that the Harley-Davidson would win first, second, fourth, fifth, sixth and seventh again this year, same as last, but you can bet your last buffalo that the sender of every one of these telegrams asking for results knew that a Harley-Davidson victory would be the news flashed on the afternoon of the fourth from Dodge City.

"Yank" and his $800 smile

But the Harley-Davidson did more. Not satisfied with winning the race the Gray Fellow lowered every record. Irving Janke took first place in 3 hours, forty-five minutes and thirty-six seconds. Otto Walker's time on a Harley-Davidson when he lowered the Dodge City record last year was 3:55:45. Think of it, Janke pranced around that track with the temperature somewhere around 110 in the shade just 10 minutes and 9 seconds faster than Walker's record that everybody thought last year would stand for a long time to come.

But look what Floyd Clymer, the Greeley, Col., boy did to the 100-mile record established by Carl Goudy last year, 1:14:10. Clymer's time this year on a Harley-Davidson was 1:11:45, or 2 minutes and 25 seconds faster. The

Systematic checking part of team work spirit at Dodge City

record for the 200-mile distance had been held by Otto Walker, the time being 2:32:58. Janke's new record made this year is 2:27:22, or 5 minutes and 36 seconds faster. The time made by Clymer this year of 71 minutes and 45 seconds for the hundred is absolutely the fastest time for that distance ever made on a dirt track and even beats the time made by Armstrong on the Tacoma board track of 1:13:41 4-5. Clymer's average was 83.62 miles an hour.

Not the least of the long list of notable accomplishments of the Harley-Davidson at Dodge City was the fact that Ray Weishaar on a stock pocket valve motored Gray Fellow captured third place in 3:55:53 and defeated his old rival, "Speck" Warner, who finished fourth, 4:16:17.

Tire trouble and a change of spark plugs, aside from his regular stops for fuel lost many precious minutes for Weishaar in enforced lingering at the pits. Were it not for this hoodoo Ray might have been able to make it a one, two victory for the Harley-Davidson. As it was, Weishaar made a tremendous show-

ing in increased speed over the big valve and eight-valve racers of other makes that trailed behind him at the finish in spite of the time he was forced to make up due to losses of time at the pits.

The battle between Clymer and Janke for first place furnished some of the greatest thrills in this year's classic. The two Harley-Davidson riders rode neck and neck mile after mile, alternating in the lead, before Clymer dropped out in the 108th lap, giving the Milwaukee boy a clear field for the $800 hung up, $600 for first place and $200 for breaking the 200-mile mark. The excessive speed bottled up in Janke's mount was shown repeatedly during the course of the Dodge City race when the old fox, Joe Wolter, tried to hang in Janke's suction and only was successful for short intervals when the kid would pull away.

Floyd Clymer, Greeley, Col.

The Harley-Davidson Enthusiast

Elsa of 1920.

cooperation of every town through which we passed. Police protection was always assured.

These road races were discontinued in the early twenties after the Denver Post had sponsored a three-corner road race between a special train, automobiles and motorcycles. The special train was and still is an annual feature sponsored by the Denver *Post* carrying prominent Coloradians from Denver to the annual Frontier Days Celebration at Cheyenne.

Most interesting of all early day road races (which actually was one against time) was one in which I took part. In 1915 a publicity stunt was thought up that created the re-enactment of the famous early day Pony Express. The Federation of American Motorcyclists, in cooperation with the United States Government and the Panama-Pacific Exposition in San Francisco, conducted this longest of all American speed races, from Washington, D.C. to San Francisco. In each state riders were selected to carry a message in a leather case from President Woodrow Wilson to the President of the Panama-Pacific Exposition at San Francisco. The message was to be carried day and night by motorcyclists, and riders of all makes were selected. Unfortunately, the message hit San Francisco about four days late, due to bad storms in the Midwest.

Road racing without doubt does develop not only better handling motorcycles but more efficient transmissions, engines, tires, ignitions and other things necessary in the designing of better and more efficient motorcycles for the average rider. — F.C.

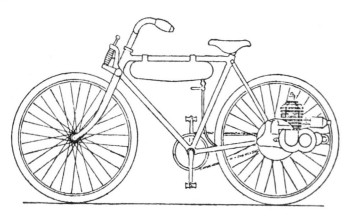

Tavernier 1920 Bicycle Motor.

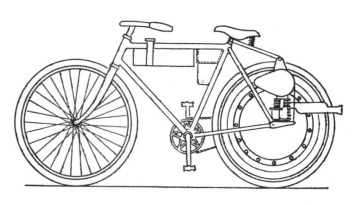

French Voisin of 1920.

William Davidson, in side car, and William S. Harley were great sportsmen, and apparently good fishermen, as evidenced by this photo. They often rode motorcycles into the backwoods country.

French Lumen scooter of 1920.

French Peugeot of 1920 with front wheel engine.

Left to right—Arthur Davidson, Walter Davidson, William S. Harley, and William Davidson at end of assembly line to see a new model finished and ready for the crate.

The famous British Brough-Superior which belonged to Lawrence of Arabia.

Art Goebel in his Travel Air monoplane, "The Woolaroc," with which he won the Dole Race to Honolulu from Oakland. He was the first man to fly from the U.S. mainland to Honolulu. Goebel is a former motorcycle racer from Colorado. He is shown astride a 1930 Harley-Davidson, at the Denver Airport. The Harley dealer, Floyd Clymer, at right.

Walter Davidson, of Harley-Davidson Motor Company, was in Japan in 1930. Alf Child took this photo of him astride a 1912 Harley-Davidson. It was taken in front of the Harley-Davidson agency in Tokyo. The bike was made before Walter was born.

Shown here are members of the Chinese Army in North China and Manchuria. Hundreds of Harley-Davidsons were sold from 1928 to 1930 to the Chinese Armies in North China. Many were captured by the Japanese after Chang-Tso-Lin was killed. These two Chinese soldiers were photographed by the then Harley-Davidson representative in Manchuria, Alf Child.

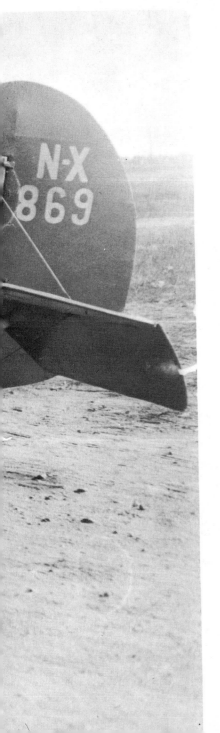

for Service!

Indian MOTOCYCLE

equipment . . . the latest — *fifty more Indians for Los Angeles.*

Indian Scout

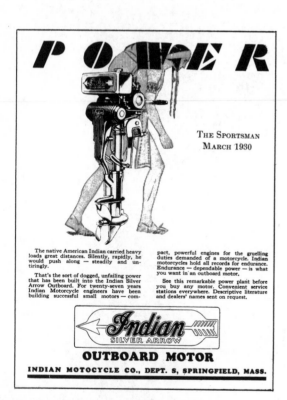

THE SPORTSMAN
MARCH 1930

The native American Indian carried heavy loads great distances. Silently, rapidly, he would push along — steadily and untiringly.

That's the sort of dogged, unfailing power that has been built into the Indian Silver Arrow Outboard. For twenty-seven years Indian Motorcycle engineers have been building successful small motors — compact, powerful engines for the gruelling duties demanded of a motorcycle. Indian motorcycles hold all records for endurance. Endurance — dependable power — is what you want in an outboard motor.

See this remarkable power plant before you buy any motor. Convenient service stations everywhere. Descriptive literature and dealers' names sent on request.

Indian SILVER ARROW

OUTBOARD MOTOR

INDIAN MOTOCYCLE CO., DEPT. S, SPRINGFIELD, MASS.

Indian 4

Indian 74

Buy the one machine that gives *real* service—INDIAN.

SPRINGFIELD, MASSACHUSETTS

In 1954, this unique Sunbeam 500cc overhead valve Twin was popular.

This 1934 350cc Jawa Twin was built in Czechoslovakia. (Below, left)

In 1930, the winner of the annual Jack Pine Endurance Run, held at Lansing, Michigan, was young Bill Davidson, who is now President of the Harley-Davidson Company. (Below, right)

Probably the world's most famous motorcycle stunt man was "Putt" Mossman, shown here with his wife in 1935 on his world tour. At left is Alf Child, then Harley-Davidson representative in Japan. (Bottom)

SIX CYLINDER INDIAN, *Wichita, Kansas. Amusement Park owner, Herb Ottoway, is a skilled machinist and collector and restorer of antique cars, and an enthusiastic motorcyclist. Shown here is the only 6-cylinder motorcycle ever manufactured, and it was by Ottoway, not Indian. Herb took two 4-cylinder Indian engines, cut them in half, made all of the necessary equipment shown—such as the crankcase, crankshaft, exhaust and intake manifolds— and built this unique bike, using Harley-Davidson front forks. This beautiful showpiece had two interesting instrument panels—one mounted on the tank, and the other on the handlebars. The bike also has a Motorola radio. Herb calls his bike the "Super 600 HJO."*

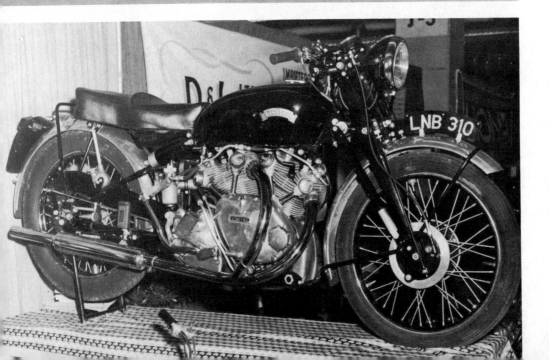

One of the excellent big British motorcycles was this 1952 Series C Vincent Rapide. It was a 61-cubic-inch Twin.

This 1940 Crocker "61 Twin" was built by Al Crocker in Los Angeles. Crocker also built a very fine scooter with a Lauson engine. After about four years, Mr. Crocker discontinued manufacturing, as his costs for custom-made limited production units were too high to compete with the large manufacturers. (Top, left and right)

Collecting and restoring motorcycles is a fast-growing hobby in the U.S. Ted Hodgdon, shown here with his 1912 4-cylinder Henderson and his 1914 B.S.A. single. (Bottom, left and right)

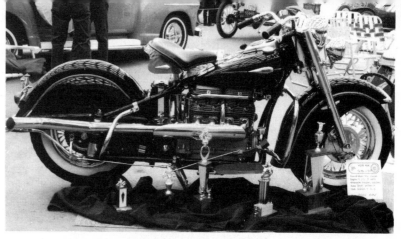

This restored 1942 Indian "4," owned by Edward Wolski, won second place for best restoration at Autorama, held at Cobo Hall in Detroit in 1965.

*Irene Dunne and Cary Grant in "The
Awful Truth."*

*Betty Hutton, in "The Perils of
Pauline," used an Indian. She dis-
mounts from her Indian to climb a
rope ladder below an airplane.*

Roy Rogers (who is a motorcycle rider and owner) and his horse "Trigger."

Martha Raye has fun ticketing Officer Ellis in the "College Holiday" film.

Ginger Rogers comforts Burgess Meredith in R.K.O. film, where 1938 Indian Dispatch-Tow 3-wheeler was used.

Janet Blair, Brian Aherne and Rosalind Russell as they appeared in Columbia production, "My Sister Eileen," on a Gaynor Scooter unit.

Spencer Tracey and Dickie Moore in "Disorderly Conduct."

When George M. Hendee and Oscar Hedstrom teamed up to build the first Indian motorcycle at Springfield, Massachusetts, little did they dream of the present-day machine, and the hundreds of innovations and changes that have taken place throughout the years. Back in 1901, they were not quite sure of the name that their strange creation should bear.

As early as 1895, in the first issue of *Horseless Age*, four-wheeled vehicles were not then called automobiles, but carried such names as kerosene carriage, electric wagon, motor road wagon, petroleum carriage, vapor-driven horseless carriage, motor trap, motor drag, business wagon, steam carriage, ether bicycle, and last, but of real importance, was the name to be applied to the powered two-wheeler which we refer to today as the motorcycle. No less than six three-wheelers and five four-wheelers were called "Motocycles."

Some of these early makes bearing the monicker of "motocycle" were Victoria, Holmes, Salisbury, Buckeye, Sturges, Lewis and Tinkham. These strange contraptions, even in 1895, were powered by every conceivable method — steam, kerosene, electricity, hot air and even by means of a spring. It was not until about 1899 that the word "automobile" replaced the word "motocycle" with many of the pioneers. Perhaps Hendee and Hedstrom figured they had won at least a moral victory by calling their Indian a "Motocycle." Indian was known for many years as the Indian "Motocycle" (spelled without the letter "r").

Not until after Hendee and Hedstrom had dis-

When I was fourteen years old I learned to ride a motorcycle backward, and I never forgot how. Photo was taken in 1953 on a Triumph.

posed of their interest in the Hendee Manufacturing Company (later changed to Indian Motocycle Company) did they give up the name "Motocycle." In the early years many persons thought the word misspelled without the letter "r" appearing, but the founders of Indian felt that the name was a valuable trademark.

Throughout the years, changes came about that revolutionized the motorcycle business. Between 1900 and 1910 the great battle raged between chain- and belt-driven machines. Indian, strongest exponent of the chain drive, even succumbed against the will of Engineer Hedstrom, and at different times Indian machines were offered with V belts and flat belts. They even went so far as to build some machines with the front pulley and the rear pulley of almost equal sizes. Internal reduction gears were used on these models. To try to improve on the chain-drive unit they once made a machine with a front gear drive — that is to say, without a front chain but a roller drive to the countershaft. It was noisy and troublesome. The compensating sprocket, once used to smooth out operation of the chain-driven machines, was later replaced by what was first called a "Free Engine Clutch."

Operated by hand, this clutch enabled the engine to be started with the rear wheel off the ground. By applying the clutch gently, the machine got under way. The method was almost identical to starting in high gear on present models—a rather slow process. The clutch took an awful beating, and "clutch slipping" to get over a steep hill or ride on a muddy road became quite an art.

At the Suzuki Test Track in Japan, Floyd Clymer is shown alongside factory tester, then takes a spin on the banked track and tries out a Suzuki riding backwards around the track.

One of the early jokes they tell is about a farmer lad who went to the city to buy a motorcycle. The salesman carefully explained all about the machine and wound up by saying, "And don't forget, we now have a free engine." The country chap replied, "If the engine is free, how much does the rest of it cost?" An early Indian Branch Manager named Johnson, in Denver, Colorado, often told that story.

Another battle was the one between automatic and mechanical intake valves. Early makes had an automatic intake that opened by the suction of the piston going down on the induction stroke. Automatic intakes were tricky devices, and a sort of snorting or snoring noise usually occurred at slow speeds. The mechanical intake operated by a cam and push rod soon replaced the automatic.

In 1912, Indian introduced a two-speed gear box, countershaft-mounted, and in 1914 Harley-Davidson offered a new model with a two-speed transmission mounted in the rear hub. The clutch was located inside the rear sprocket unit. Reading-Standard, a really worthwhile pioneer, came out with a single-chain drive and internal gear primary drive.

The slogan of the R-S was "Built and Tested in the Mountains," the factory being located in hilly Pennsylvania at Reading. Jokesters referred to it as being "Built in the Mountains and tested down hill."

Wagner, a pioneer from St. Paul, once built a motorcycle with two single-cylinder engines mounted tandem-style in a frame that seated two persons, fore and aft, like a tandem bicycle. Two flat belts were used, and the makers claimed that one belt could be disengaged so that one engine only could be used on level roads and both engines hooked up when the going got tough.

A unique early effort was the Militaire, with wooden artillery wheels and a shaft drive in a four-cylinder job. The single-cylinder Militaire had a chain for final drive and a friction transmission.

The early drip-style oilers were replaced by mechanical oilers and they were gear driven. Electric lights replaced the gas generator, and also the very popular Prest-O-Lite tank that adorned the handle bars of many a motorbike even as late as 1919.

Two-cycle jobs were offered by many, including Indian, Excelsior, Schickel, Cleveland, Evans and others. Indian once had a tiny opposed twin known as the model "O"—it was terribly underpowered and soon became known as the "Model Nothing." Harley-Davidson gave the opposed twin idea a try with their Sport Model 37-cubic-inch twin. Thor cut some ice at one time by building a motorcycle painted white, with an internal reduction gear and single chain drive. V-shaped handle bars were an early Thor trademark. And Yale once announced to the world that they had licked the cooling problem by locating the cooling fins on their cylinders cast in a horizontal line so that the air would flow through the fins freely.

Racing boomed prior to and immediately after the First World War. The early racing machines were known as open-ported jobs. They had holes drilled in the cylinder at a point directly above the piston top when it was as far down as possible. Oil and smoke poured out of the holes and the roar made them sound even faster than they were.

Indian and Merkel had been the top-notch ported jobs, until along came Excelsior with new and fast models. They secured such then-famous riders as Don Johns, Morty Graves, Lee Humiston, Joe Wolter and Erle (Pop) Armstrong. The days of the ported jobs were before Harley-Davidson built machines for competition.

When the open port jobs passed out, new and faster "closed port" machines came into vogue. Harley-Davidson startled the world with the speed of their pocket-valve engines. Indian produced fast 4-valve singles and 8-valve twins (two intakes and two exhaust valves per cylinder). These valves were of different sizes and mounted in the roof of a flat overhead unit. Harley-Davidson countered with dual valve machines, having a roof-type head similar to modern overhead valve machines. Excelsior did them both one better by building a big valve job, and I do mean *big* valve engine. The valves were 2¼ inches in diameter. These jobs were quite fast for pocket-valve motors, and such riders as Bob Perry, Carl Goudy, Glen Stokes and others won many long-distance races with this type of engine. In 1916, I won the first motorcycle hillclimb up Pikes Peak with one of these big valved Excelsior engines. Excelsior then built a roof-type single-valve overhead job and experimented with an overhead cam-shaft model. Later, Excelsior, under the skilled direction of engineer A. R. Constantine (later Director of Engineering at Indian) put out a 45-cubic-inch overhead-valve job that cleaned up *all* the hillclimb contests. "Thanks," Mr. Constantine says, "to the riding of Joe Petrali."

The roads in those days were not too good. Once five riders, including myself, started from Denver to the Motorcycle Show in Chicago. We had single-speed Excelsiors. It rained nearly every day. We broke spokes; the clutches got red hot from slipping in the mud. We rode the railroad tracks at times, and it took us five days to get from Denver to Des Moines, Iowa, about 850 miles. We left the machines there and went on to Chicago by train.

I've enjoyed every year of my motorcycling experiences. People used to remark to me, "What do you see in those things?" Every real dyed-in-the-wool motorcyclist knows what I mean when I say it's a difficult problem to explain to others just why we have enjoyed the sport of motorcycling. I'd say that it is a hobby and a sport that gets into a fellow's blood. It's the same enthusiasm that makes a fisherman what he is, a golfer enjoy his game, a stamp collector his hobby. Motorcycling is truly a wonderful sport . . . it is splendid recreation . . . and it is healthful. I've found the great majority of motorcycle riders to be real fellows—good friends and pals. In my many experiences with motorcycle riders through the years, I've made some wonderful acquaintances and life-long friends that I should never have known had we not had a common interest—motorcycling.—F.C.

This photo, taken at Wembley Stadium in London in 1937, shows from left to right: Wilbur Lamoreaux, second place, Jack Milne, first place, third place winner Cordy Milne, and Britisher Jack Parker, who won fourth. The Milne brothers and Lamoreaux were the three Americans who won first, second and third before 100,000 spectators.

Lionel Van Praag, congratulates Milne, 1937 Champion .

Auto Cycle Union official congratulates new champion, as 1936 champion, Bluey Wilkson, looks on.

When short track (speedway) motorcycle racing reached its peak in California in the mid-thirties, three outstanding riders were developed—Cordy Milne, Wilbur Lamoreaux and Jack Milne, all of Pasadena, Calif. They were all friends and were motorcycle messengers for Western Union. Soon after starting to race they showed exceptional ability. Both Lammy and Cordy won A.M.A. American Championships. Jack, along with brother Cordy, and Lammy started dominating the races on the West Coast. In 1937 they went to Australia, and later to England, where they became stars against the foreigners. In 1937, before 100,000 people at Wembley Stadium in London, this trio won first, second and third in the World's Speedway Championship. At that time there were seven tracks (operating every night) in London and the three Americans were the sensation and they became team captains of three of the London tracks. Lammy won second and Cordy won third in the World's title event. In 1939 when war broke out, they returned to the States and continued to dominate short track events on the West Coast.

Near the end of World War II these three, along with another friend and racer, Jimmy Gibb —and with Floyd Clymer as business manager— formed the Lincoln Park Speedway Association and promoted highly successful short track racing for several years in Los Angeles and Santa Monica.

Later they started in business. Lammy (with the Milne brothers as partners) started his own cycle business in Glendale. He died on May 11, 1963 and his wife, Margaret, still operates the dealership. The Milne brothers have expanded in Pasadena, and now have one of the largest motorcycle, bicycle and automobile businesses in the West. Their buildings and lots cover a two-block area. Former hillclimb champion, Gene Rhyne, is motorcycle shop foreman. They also operate a successful wholesale motorcycle supply business, with Andy Andrews as the manager. They handle BSA, BMW, Yamaha, are U.S. distributors for the Austrian Puch motorcycles; and Plymouth, Jeep, Peugeot, Toyota and Renault, with Bob Feuerhelm as car manager, his brother Pete as service manager, and his brother Harvey as parts manager. All of these men are former motorcyclists and long time friends of the Milnes.

p.s.

Always at press time there are late arrivals for inclusion in any publication. Shown here are four new models which we are including on this special page, as the information arrived too late to include in the proper section.

Testi 50cc & 90cc (Italy)

Twelve different models comprise the Testi lightweight motorcycle line. Engines are 2-strokes in 50cc and 90cc sizes. Most outstanding feature of these machines is the beautiful finish. Strikingly attractive metallic paint jobs are enhanced by a "sculptured" look on fuel tanks and fenders. The "Telstar" model is the top-of-the-line production road racer, suitable for street or track. Performance is very good. The "Trail King" is Testi's bid for that booming facet of the market. It features knobby tires, plenty of chrome, and protective tubing surrounding the headlight. Fan-cooling protects against overheating under severe engine loads. There are many different models and all specifications are not yet available.

Harley-Davidson M-50 (U.S.A)

This new Harley-Davidson Sport M-50 is a new design in that it has a different frame and gas tank than previous models, and it has an increase of 30% in the 2-stroke engine.

Honda 450 (Japan)

This is the machine that riders and dealers of both lightweight and large machines have been anxiously awaiting. It is Honda's largest model. It is the first effort by a major lightweight manufacturer to branch out from the "fun" riding field into the realm of serious high-speed motorcycling. Although the engine is smaller than others in the "big bike" class, its status is enhanced by the fact that it has double overhead camshafts, an extremely efficient valvegear design. It is a relatively heavy bike, still unusually agile. Outstanding features include the electric starter, 12-volt electrical system, and rubber-mounted twin carburetors. The 450 also features an extremely large gasoline tank (4.2 gallons). Claimed top speed is 112 mph.

SPECIFICATIONS: Engine type— 2-cylinder, 4-stroke; Displacement—444cc (27.17 cubic inches); Bore & stroke—70mm x 57.8mm; Horsepower—43 @ 8500 rpm; Starting system—electric & kick; Transmission—4-speed; Weight— 412 lbs.

Laverda 200cc (Italy)

Most Italian motorcycles are constructed of parts produced by several major firms who build standardized frames, engines, suspension units, wheels, etc. The Laverda is unique in that it is built, for the most part, "from the ground up." The manufacturer is a leading Italian aircraft producer who has decided to make a bid for a share of the booming motorcycle market. Many features are unconventional and precision is evident throughout. The 4-stroke overhead valve engine features ample use of alloy, including cylinder head and block. Transmission is 4-speed with a single plate cone clutch. 85 mph is claimed, along with superb handling and stability.

SPECIFICATIONS: Engine—4-stroke 200cc OHV; Transmission— 4-speed; Clutch—single plate cone type; Frame—combination tubular and pressed steel; Suspension— Laverda's own design front fork, Ceriani rear suspension; Weight 256 lbs.

the end